A GUIDE TO

Victorian Antiques

With Notes on the

Early Nineteenth Century

by

Raymond F. and Marguerite W. Yates

Drawings and (most) photographs
by the authors

GRAMERCY PUBLISHING COMPANY
NEW YORK

Dedicated To

Jack Deeringer and Ethel Carnochan

who helped us learn

to appreciate old things

CONTENTS

Foreword   *Dear Reader:*   xi

I. What Do You Mean, Victorian?   1

II. Provincial Victorian and a Guide to Age   26

III. Victorian and Early Nineteenth Century
     Chairs   49

IV. Victorian Chests and Secretaries   82

V. Tables   109

VI. What the Victorians Slept On   125

VII. Lamps and Lighting   135

VIII. Clocks   156

IX. Mirrors   174

X. Victorian Pictures   180

XI. China   192

XII. Glassware   208

XIII. Silver, Pewter, and Britannia Ware   228

ACKNOWLEDGMENTS

The writers wish to acknowledge with gratitude the kindnesses of the following people who supplied either photographs or data or both for use in the present book: Leon and Sophie Frank, of the Olde Lamps, Inc., Buffalo, N.Y.; Mrs. Penn Perkins, antique dealer, Molyneaux Corners, N.Y.; Mrs. George Carnochan of Lewiston Heights, N.Y.; Arnold MacDonald, Advertising Department, International Silver Company; John E. O'Donnell, Reed and Barton; Florence E. Wright, New York State College of Home Economics, Ithaca, N.Y.; Charles F. Campbell, Grand Rapids Furniture Museum, Grand Rapids, Michigan.

FOREWORD

Dear Reader:

If you are in search of a Goddard block-front desk, a set of Philadelphia Chippendale chairs, or a Duncan Phyfe sofa, this is not your book. If you collect Chinese porcelains, Bentley basalt busts, oriental Lowestoft punch bowls, Chantilly snuff boxes, Chelsea figurines, or Baccarat candelabra; again, this is not your book. Rather this book has been written for a class of collectors who have never had a book of their own; a book that would for the first time tell them something about the things that they can afford to collect rather than the things they can only dream about or see in the windows of the smart shops or in museums.

Through a curious oversight on the part of publishers, the books dealing with antiques consist of matter that interests only ten per cent or less of the people who collect antiques or near-antiques. The remaining ninety per cent of the collectors have been left to shift for themselves and to find their information where they may. At least so it was with the authors who for ten long years searched the meager records for cogent and informative guidance in assembling a collection of Early and Mid-Victorian furniture and accessories. The carefully sifted product of their labors is now in your hands and they hope that it will be useful to you.

It was indeed only while the authors' work was in progress that Early Victorian gained its majority in point of time and was permitted, grudgingly no doubt on the part of some, to enter the sanctified realm of antiques. Yes, there have been and still are cat-calls and derisive remarks from the snooty connoisseurs, but the fact remains that the era of Early Victorian Americana has finally come into its own both by way of public acclaim and interest and by having achieved its one hundredth Birthday—the arbitrary rule by which the relics of bygone days reach a certain respectability whether they have earned it or not.

Indeed the furniture relics of Colonial America suffered the same indignities until the display at the Philadelphia Centennial in 1876 brought them down out of dusty attics and haymows to serve again the purposes for which they were made. Perhaps it does not need to be said that sound investments in the better things that the early Victorians used will gain both in value and in respectability as the years pass just as in the case of Colonial things which were all but forgotten in the flood of cheap machine-made furniture that swept the country after the Civil War.

Inasmuch as Victorian articles have finally reached antique-hood, the authors have thought that the best way to celebrate might be a practical book devoted to their collection.

Here, too, the authors would like to say a word or two about dealers in antiques. The intense public interest generated within the past few years has brought a great horde of unqualified opportunists into the field. And why not?

The requirements for a dealership in antiques are delightfully simple. A capital of a few hundred dollars, an empty room, attic, or barn, an old spinning wheel for the lawn, and a subscription to the trade magazines are among the chief requirements. And the shop, of course, must also have a quaint name, such as the Black Bonnet, The Cracked Crock, or the Old Stone Whatsit. Given such assets, many people throughout the land have established themselves as authorities on all sorts of antiquities ranging from Empire furniture to Wedgwood and from Wedgwood to Sheffield plate. It matters little so long as one is recognized as a "dealer."

Such people hurt and embarrass honorable men and women in the trade who seek to purchase good things at fair prices and pass them on to their clientele at reasonable profit. The old, established dealers spend much of their time seeking out desirable articles, whereas the "gold rushers" push doorbells indiscriminately always hoping to lay hold of a $50 item for $3.50, as often as not from some poor unsuspecting grandmother or housewife. If the colossal nerve of these speculators were matched by their knowledge of antiques, the trade at large would be handsomely enriched. The truth is that many of them do not know a really valuable antique when it strikes them fairly between the eyes. When they leave the range of lady's and gentleman's chairs, late Victorian glassware, late Victorian chests, and the ugly oil lamps of the late nineteenth century, they are pretty much at sea.

The shop chatter of these new arrivals runs about the same the country over. "This is a fine old piece" and "This is a collector's item" are stock phrases, and "This is a museum piece" has grown to be a nauseating bromide. If our museums were cluttered up with all of the miscellaneous junk alleged by ignorant dealers to be candidates for museums, the number of museums in the country would have to be tripled. The bold and careless use of the phrase has, however, cinched many sales and captured much juicy profit. Mrs. Jones, her interest newly awakened, seems to have a pathetic respect for the pontifical judgment of people whose sole training amounts to an avid reading of the trade magazine Hobbies, which reading is done not so much for learning more about the trade as for keeping informed about the current prices that are asked by mail order competitors. It is all very racket-like and amusing.

It probably does not occur to the pretender mouthing the "museum piece" phrase that museums are not always interested in rarities and are never interested in curios or oddities unless they touch the life of some famous person or event in which a museum might be interested. A grandfather's clock that fed the bird, started the morning coffee, and reminded one of the anniversary of the Battle of Waterloo might well be the only clock of its kind in the world, but that would make it rare only in a very limited sense. When the careful and able staff of the Metropolitan Museum of Art set up its Victorian rooms, it sought no rarities. Rather it sought good typical things of the Early Victorian period; things like Belter sofas and side chairs, a rosewood square piano, a carved center table, and oval gilded frames. It was good Victorian stuff but not necessarily rare.

Most of these "museum pieces" now offered were the products of a new and careless world ushered in by the machine age. Much of the truck and trash that age produced is now feverishly sought after by people who should know better, but never will until their little world of spurious treasures is appraised anew at more reasonable levels.

Museum pieces, indeed! The authors' own home should be bulging with them because they have been offered so many golden opportunities. However, by and large, they have avoided dealers who have too many such doubtful wares. The museum-piece palaver is Number 1 on the list of things that dealers do who should be avoided. The remainder of the list follows:

2. On the whole the authors are suspicious of people who allege they "had to pay" such-and-such a price for an article they wish to sell at only a ten per cent profit.

3. The authors rarely if ever purchase an article when a dealer lowers his original price. That is usually the they-may-be-suckers approach and they resent the insinuation.

4. The authors purchase antiques only and not the stories that go with them.

5. They prefer to deal in shops where articles bear price tags and they do not like to feel they are being "measured" when they enter a shop. Having ordinary middle-class pride in their personal appearance, they do not feel that it should be used against them. Whether justifiable or not, they are very suspicious of dealers who upon being asked for the price say, "Well, I'll have to get ———— for that." They have no interest whatsoever in what a dealer paid for an article so long as its quoted price is fair.

6. They prefer to be told of imperfections and repairs in a straightforward manner and they highly respect the dealer who does not wait for the detection of these by the purchaser. Here one must be careful to see that a minor defect is not pointed out to avoid detection of a major one.

But what, one rightfully asks, is an antique? Today this term stands as one of the most abused words in the English language. Although the position taken is purely arbitrary, it may be generally assumed that an antique is something at least a hundred years old. That appears to be a generally accepted requirement for antiquity. This does not mean, however, that all desirable collectibles are that old and that if they are not that old, they should not be purchased as valuable Americana. The fact is that many or even most of the small and so-called antique shops of the day have very few if any actual antiques on display. The point to be borne in mind is that not all things antique by right of age are beautiful or desirable and that not all things not dignified by the term are trash. Ultimately, decisions depend upon the training, the desires, the fancies, and the feeling for artistic subtleties possessed by the collector.

RAYMOND F. YATES
MARGUERITE W. YATES

Lockport, New York, 1949

CHAPTER I

What Do You Mean, Victorian?

VICTORIAN as applied to antiques is a big word. It may include any article of American or English furniture, art, bric-a-brac, china, silverware, or glassware produced between the years 1837, when the shy little Queen climbed to her throne, and 1901 when, as a tough and venerated old lady, she left it in death. Victoria's reign not only witnessed the final flowering of British imperialism but, more important still, it witnessed the industrial revolution which created both the English and American middle classes and sealed the doom of many craftsmen whether they were shoemakers, glass blowers, leather-dressers or cabinetmakers. Styles, designs, methods —all suffered through many changes and what passed for improvement. In so far as furniture was concerned, the fine traditions of cabinetmaking began to go down in a blizzard of sawdust and chips.

Victorian Americana, in which our prime interest lies, went from *A* to *Izzard* in design. It was influenced by practically everything that went before it and it had very little to call its own. In many respects it was a period of stagnation with little that was in good taste and with but few things that were genuinely beautiful. This was the age in America during which the great middle class was in the process of formation and when wealth began to reach the hands of uncultured people. They were the aggressive entrepreneurs, the mercantile people who suddenly developed a vague yearning for elegance and had nothing but money with which to satisfy it. It was this untutored indulgence more than anything else that brought

1

forth many of the monstrosities so characteristic of the Victorian transformation.

Coarse people suddenly grown rich gladly accepted anything so long as they thought it to be in vogue. The furniture products of the time were rhapsodies in wood involving confused Greek forms, Turkish opulence, Venetian and Florentine extravagance, Napoleonic Empire with Egyptian motifs, and Louis XV, to say nothing of passing fads sponsored by the later (1870's) manufacturers of furniture. Such articles of furniture were set in high ceilinged rooms with loud floral wall coverings, Axminster rugs, heavy tasseled draperies, and a wholesale use of brocades, damasks, satins, and horsehair cloth. Woods in vogue were walnut, mahogany, rose, and an occasional piece of ebony. Mauve, lilac, purple, blue, deep purple, brown, and red formed the range of popular colors.

A few individualists attempted to hold out against the Victorian flood, stubborn old Duncan Phyfe among them. Even he finally had to give up in despair during the middle 1840's and retire to putter with his beloved tools in a backyard workshop. Some cabinetmakers among the lesser lights either hired out to those employing machinery or purchased such machinery themselves and set about making "store furniture." Still others refused to bow to the power machines with their hissing steam engines and flapping leather belts. They went on producing handmade furniture in their little shops, and not a small number of furniture retailers maintained a cabinet department in charge of a craftsman who catered to individual tastes and from whom came some of the best-made furniture that the Early and Mid-Victorian era had to offer. Also for many years the old craft of joinery still flourished in the hinterlands of America, supplying the simple needs of the provinces well into the 1880's—but of that, more later.

Among the few who left a definite, traceable mark on the furniture of the Early Victorian period, we find John Hall, a Baltimore architect. In 1840, he published his *Cabinet Makers' Assistant* wherein he pictured the creations of a not-too-artistic mind. Whatever else might be said about Hall's doubtful contributions to early Victorian art, the fact remains that his furniture designs enjoyed a ten-year vogue and that his was one of the major impacts on the Early Victorian era. He had departed from the deeply carved mahogany surfaces and favored massiveness with long, flowing curves obviously borrowed from the Louis XV period. His inspiration for massiveness, if such it may be called, came from the Late American Empire period which was then drawing to a close. This was the period when great chunks of mahogany were carved with acanthus leaves for the posts of beds and the pilasters of heavy chests, the

DESIGNED, DRAWN AND PUBLISHED, BY JOHN HALL, ARCHITECT.
BALTIMORE

Fig. 1. The title page of John Hall's *The Cabinet Makers' Assistant*, the book that set American furniture styles between the years 1840 and 1850.

latter with clawed feet which presented a curious admixture of details from the vegetable and animal kingdoms. Some people place Hall's creations within the class of Late American Empire and, so far as massiveness is concerned, there is some excuse for this otherwise loose association.

The Hall era was also noted for its extensive use of mahogany and (later) rosewood veneer. Factories producing such furniture must have smeared glue about with reckless abandon. All of the large scrolls were veneer-covered on all sides and all large flat surfaces were also covered. In fact most Hall furniture was practically incased in veneer; its skin looked expensive but inside it was pretty cheap and shoddy stuff.

The people who insist upon referring to Hall furniture as "Late Empire" may in a sense be correct. Certainly the elephantine features of Empire had not yet been cast off. What Hall himself thought can easily be imagined. Clearly he was an opportunist. Late American Empire was expensive, as might be expected of furniture so deeply and elaborately carved. Then came the band saw capable of turning sharp curves even in thick pieces of wood. Curves are decorative. Why, then, Hall must have thought, would it not be possible to re-establish Empire using the saw and the curve rather than the hand chisel and the acanthus leaf? That was a thought that had more commercial logic than artistic logic. Every furniture factory from Cincinnati to Boston that had one of the newfangled band saws set about making Hall's furniture. The whole case rested on the economics of low-cost production, and Hall made himself important to the history of American furniture. His motive was clear as, may be gained from reading the preface in his book, *The Cabinet Makers' Assistant* (Baltimore, 1840). This is quoted below:

> Novelty, simplicity and practicability, are blended with the present designs, in which originality mostly prevails; a few of those designs have been taken from work previously executed, in consequence of their being highly approved. As far as possible, the style of the United States is blended with European taste, and a graceful outline and simplicity of parts are depicted in all the objects. The present work will not only be useful to the manufacturer, but of great importance to persons who may order furniture as they will be enabled to select their patterns and have them executed without any misunderstanding. The great variety of scrolls shown in this work, with instructions for drawing them, will afford great facilities to the artizan in applying them to a great variety of work not enumerated in the present collection. The short treatise on perspective will be found of the utmost

FIG. 2. Drawings from John Hall's book, *The Cabinet Makers' Assistant*, published in Baltimore, Maryland, in 1840. Hall's designs were in vogue for over ten years and many pieces of his heavy furniture are still to be found about the country. The heavy scrolls so characteristic of Hall furniture were made possible by the then-newly invented, steam-driven bandsaws. Some still refer to this furniture as Late Empire, but this is a loose use of the term.

importance to every cabinet-maker, as they can acquire, by a very little study of these principles, a sufficient knowledge to enable them to draw with accuracy any piece of work that may present itself to their mind. Throughout the whole of the designs in this work, particular attention has been bestowed in an economical arrangement to save labor; which being an important point, is presumed will render the collection exceedingly useful to the cabinet-maker.

John Hall,
Architect.

Perhaps it was Hall's designs more than any other that prompted Phyfe to refer to the "butcher furniture" of the 1840's. That such furniture became popular is easy to understand. It had a pseudo-elegance about it and was large and expensive looking, while it really was not too expensive at all, because more than any other formal furniture produced for the growing American middle class *up to that time*, it was a product of the machine, the machine being a combination of the factory-introduced steam engine, the circular saw, and the band saw.

Side by side with Hall's clumsy innovations, so eagerly produced by the small furniture factories and individual cabinetmakers of the day, there also appeared revived forms of the Louiv XV period. This happened during the reign of Louis Philippe in France and its effect was especially noticeable in chairs. It was during the 1840's that the so-called lady's and gentleman's chairs were introduced, and the influence persisted for thirty odd years. Countless thousands of these chairs were manufactured and today they more than anything else have become symbols of early Victorian times.

During the mid-1840's another stout individualist added confusion to an already confused scene. This was John Henry Belter, a Württemberg-trained mechanic and wood-carver, who set up his business at Number 40 Chatham Street in New York City in 1844 and who aimed his creations at the carriage trade. He literally carved his way to favor and fame and his pieces are today perhaps the most sought

FIG. 3. A John Belter room of the 1850's. The scrolled chair at the left of the table represents the later forms which his carving took. John Belter marked the Early and Mid-Victorian periods but not nearly so much as did his contemporary, John Hall, the Baltimore architect, whose furniture designs so neatly fitted the needs of the middle class. At least the Hall furniture was massive and expensive-looking, although its deceiving elegance was machine-produced and therefore moderately priced. (Courtesy Metropolitan Museum of Art, New York.)

after of all those by the Victorian workers. A living room in good Belter might today command as much as two or three thousand dollars. It is perhaps the scarcity of his work rather than its artistic appeal that brings such high prices. Artistically his furniture was of highly questionable value although he was a superb craftsman.

The backs and seat fronts of his earlier chairs were profusely ornamented with deep, pierced carving at which he was extremely clever. If one likes fruit and leaves issuing from cornucopias or

FIG. 4. (Left) Pier table from John Hall's sketch book. Pier tables were made for use between windows. Mirror in back permitted milady to see if her pantalets were hanging properly. (Right) A work- or sewing table designed by John Hall.

tightly arranged clusters of flowers, one will like early Belter. To more temperate tastes, however, he will be rather tiresome and gaudy and to pocketbooks suffering a degree of malnutrition, he will remain in the limbo of lost things. Belter left his mark but it was carved too deeply and it was too Germanic to interest most practical Americans. By 1850, however, his work was so popular that he had to import a number of German craftsmen and carvers to keep up with the demand.

Later on, perhaps after 1855, the year in which he pioneered plywood and patented his improvement, Belter became a little more acceptable as the public began to lose its interest in a diet of rosewood and mahogany fruit. Belter, like others, abandoned his naturalistic motifs and began producing intertwining scrolls, but he still could not resist his mania for carving. To those who enthuse over his work to the contrary notwithstanding, he must go down as merely a very good mechanic more than moderately handy with carving tools. He simply happened to have been born in an era that tolerated that sort of thing largely because it looked (and indeed was) expensive. He died in 1866, the owner of a sizable furniture factory and having chiselled his niche in Americana.

Belter was by no means the only nonconformist of his time who was able to carry his business from the Early into the Mid-Victorian period. Swanky carriage trade purchased very little of the cheaper machine-made furniture. Here and there many other able craftsmen, now nameless, labored to satisfy the expensive tastes of those who could afford the luxury of handmade articles, and from such sources have come down to us many of the choicest pieces, choice for their individuality and choice for the fine workmanship they exhibit. Thus between the 1850's and 1870 one may now and then come upon really fine articles of furniture from a constructional viewpoint. For those in search of the better things produced during these years, it is also to be noted that many of the larger and better furniture shops in the urban centers of the country sold excellent importations from both England and France.

Clearly the year 1845 or thereabouts brought to a close a neoclassic revival both as it related to architecture and to furniture. Perhaps an article published by Arthur Gilman in 1844 had something to do with the establishment of the new trend. Then, too, there was evident at this time a new restlessness, a new urge, and a growing inclination to break with the past. New facilities were available for making things, and new wealth was falling into the hands of aggressive people who became impatient and dissatisfied with what had been created by their elders.

Purporting to be a review of Shaw's book, *Rural Architecture*, Gilman's article really amounted to a thinly veiled attack upon the classic revival, the sole inspiration of the Georgian period of the last

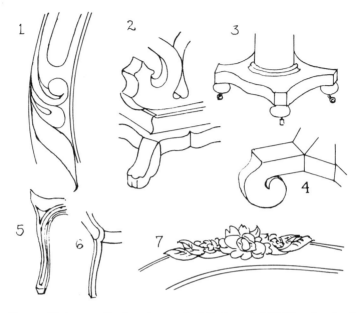

Fig. 5. Design motifs that characterized Early and Mid-Victorian furniture. (1) Finger roll carving popular during the late 1840's and to the 1860's. This carving was contemporary with fruit, flower, and nut carving. All, including finger roll, were used on chair and sofa rails. (2) Two popular features of Victorian console tables: the heavy scrolled turtle foot and the heavy scrolled pedestal with crotch mahogany veneer. (3) Pedestal and feet of a modified John Hall worktable with uncarved, mahogany-veneered column-pedestal and modified turtle bottom provided with bun feet and casters. (4) The heavy, scrolled table foot characteristic of Hall furniture. (5) The leg and knee of Early and Mid-Victorian side chairs made in cabriole style and in the Louis XV manner. (6) The cabriole side chair leg without carved or molded surfaces. (7) The type of flower carving

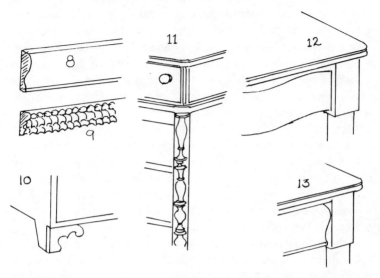

found on the top rails of many Early and Mid-Victorian parlor chairs and sofas. (8) The ogee or cyma curve often used on drawer fronts and table frames. It was invariably covered with crotch mahogany veneer. (9) So-called piecrust molding. During the 1840's a machine was invented to cut such molding. Hence molding was inexpensive and therefore used on the skirts of chests, on tables, sofa stretchers, etc. (10) The beautiful molded brackets of Chippendale finally came to this or something very similar to it during the Victorian times. (11) Many chests produced during the 1860's had chamfered (bevelled) corners to which pilasters of turned vase forms were glued. (12 and 13) Like many Empire chests, Early and Mid-Victorian chests had overhanging top drawers but were unsupported by Empire pillars or carved pilasters. These drawers were either ogee curve or serpentine, and invariably covered with crotch mahogany.

of the eighteenth century and the early part of the nineteenth century. Gilman argued for eclecticism, a new American blending of forms to create something new and distinctly American. How profoundly Gilman shook the old order is difficult to determine but his wish soon began to be fulfilled. Within the brief period of a few years a new confusion was generated. A contagious ugliness began to spread over the country, first in architecture and then in the form of furniture.

Artistically speaking, perhaps America was trying to find itself. It was then a young, lusty, and independent country and apparently it craved new things that it could at least call its own. It got them and, with few exceptions, in very bad and strictly amateur forms. This dug the grave for neo-classicism, to be sure, and it was a very sad burial even though few remained to mourn the passing.

Perhaps the beginning collector will wish to know something more about some of the details of Early and Mid-Victorian rooms. Starting with floor covering, large floral designs were great favorites in Axminster, Brussels, and Aubusson rugs. Colors inclined toward the gaudy.

Woods most favored were mahogany, rosewood (especially after 1850), and walnut. This, too, was the era of extensive veneering, a vogue poorly understood by many feminine collectors who appear to think that veneer was employed only on cheap furniture and to fool the purchaser into believing that the wood was solid mahogany or rosewood, the two early forms of veneer. The truth is that veneer was used on even the most expensive furniture and the reason is not difficult to understand. Mahogany cut from the trunk of a tree is straight-grained, uniform. On the other hand, mahogany cut from the crotches of trees exhibits the most beautiful grain patterns. Here, however, due to poor grain structure, the wood has little strength and it would be folly to use it for construction. Therefore to take advantage of its beauty, the craftsmen sliced off thin layers of it and glued it under pressure to table tops, drawer fronts, etc. It was often glued to pine or some other soft, open-grained wood because of good adhesion. Rosewood, not being

FIG. 6. An early upper-class Victorian room as assembled by the experts at the Metropolitan Museum of Art in New York City. Especially to be noted are the forms of Victorian art and picture frames. The more ordinary homes of middle-class people did not boast such heavily carved furniture, all of which was expensive. (Courtesy Metropolitan Museum of Art, New York.)

particularly strong but possessing a beautiful grain pattern, was often used as veneer.

Although not very popular among collectors but as Victorian as grandma's hoopskirt or snuffbox were the small pieces of papier-mâché furniture as often as not in the form of a tilt-top table, a sewing table, a teapoy, or a sewing box sitting on a pedestal. These were usually japanned in black or deep brown, elaborately decorated with painted and gilded ornaments with a bit of mother-of-pearl thrown in for good measure. At times the Victorians made the Florentines look like pussyfooting amateurs, and such furniture is a good instance of it.

This, too, was the era of the marble tops, many of the better class of Early Victorian parlor tables appearing with beautiful pieces of black onyx. Such tables are not to be confused with the later (after 1870) oval, oblong, and square marble-top tables that were so horribly stigmatized by the curse of Mr. Eastlake's inventions, of whom more later. Marble also came into vogue after 1865 as a covering for dressers, commodes, and wash stands, usually in its more common forms of white and brown.

This, too, was the era of the marble- or onyx-faced fireplace arranged with grates for coal burning. Such fireplaces were invariably supplied with heavily ornamented brass andirons and a gaudy coal hod japanned in black and smeared with gay flowers or chunky cherubs.

Chairs were really of many forms, although beginners appear to think that the so-called lady's and gentleman's chairs were used exclusively throughout the whole of the Victorian era. Most of the better homes had them indeed but they had other types as well. The lady's chair was especially popular because it was armless and accommodated not only the bustle and hoopskirt but also permitted milady to indulge freely in one of the ladylike pastimes of the day: tatting, knitting, or needlework. The armed gentleman's chair was not so commodious.

Victorian taste was neither all bad nor all good. No era covering a period of sixty-four years could leave a spotless record. It is conceded, however, that most by far of the artistically acceptable things that belong to the time covered by the Queen's reign were produced between the years 1837 and 1870. However, no part of the era was free of excessive ornamentation, with practically no purity of motif whatsoever, and the most fashionable of the Victorian parlors had what might be called, for want of a more adequate expression, a gay solemnity about them. The high ceilings of the rooms were usually heavily ornamented, the walls covered with gay papers, and the tall windows hung with lace curtains covered with richly colored damask or velvet drapes which excluded all but a minimum of sunlight.

Chairs and sofas were usually heavily carved, although the finger roll design was very popular on lady's and gentleman's chairs and also on side chairs and sofas. The early part of the era also brought popularity to heavily stuffed chairs done in velvet, satin, or damask and trimmed with expensive fringe. Footstools and tabourets were as likely as not covered with needle point.

Lighting fixtures between the years 1837 and 1870 covered a wide range both in design and technical quality. In the larger urban centers gas lighting was being introduced and there was also some progress in the use of inflammable liquids for lamps, sperm oil and camphene giving way to "coal oil," etc. At the same time candle-light was still in use even in the best homes, especially in bedrooms and (with elaborate candelabra) in dining rooms. Invariably one found smaller candelabra on the mantle in duplicate, usually ornamented with glass prisms. These were called girandoles.

During the early part of the era, the now-much-sought-after astral lamp was popular, with its marble base, classical brass column, glistening prisms, and frosted tulip-shaped globe. The early part of the era also witnessed the popularity of the better types of pressed Sandwich glass lamps with their ropelike wicks and sperm oil.

Many of those who assemble Early and Mid-Victorian rooms do very well on the general appointments but often err badly on wall hangings. Practically every parlor of the newly rich (and there were many of them) boasted of a family portrait or two done in

oil. During the early 1840's the daguerreotype was being introduced, and the itinerant artist or limner, and the better-established
artists who had studios in the large cities were the only sources of
family likenesses before the advent of photography. This was also
the time when the academies were teaching art to the young ladies,
and many still are the acceptable little landscapes and seascapes in
oil painted by such students. They may be found in the antique
shops of today and may be had for a few dollars each.

Although early Currier and Kellogg lithographs covering this
period are available at moderate cost, they are not acceptable in a
highly formalized Victorian room. Authentic for the period, yes,
but not authentic enough for such rooms. These early lithographers
produced art for poor families whose daughters could not attend
an academy and who did not have the money for family portraits in
oil. After all, a newly arrived entrepreneur boasting a coach and
four and an elegant new gingerbread residence on West Main
Street would consider fifty-cent pictures sold at the corner apothecary's shop quite beneath his station. This was, after all, art for the
hoi polloi.

The Mid-Victorian room will never be quite authentic unless
either a glass dome covering a group of wax flowers of a shadow
box with a garland of the same is present, whatever one may think
of them as works of art. The shadow box was a walnut frame,
square, oval, oblong or octagonal, in the center of which a deep
silk- or satin-lined box was placed, the wax flowers or other articles
being mounted in this. "Other articles" might be a home-woven
circle of human hair (usually from the deceased members of the
family) with flowers or perhaps a Parian profile in classical cameo
form.

And then there is always grandmother's whatnot with its delicate
bric-a-brac, the earlier pieces of which may be choice collectors'
items today. Here one might find plaster-of-Paris statues of Caesar,
Virgil, or Dante, Staffordshire trinket boxes, miniature china pitchers, ornate Sunday-go-to-meeting snuffboxes, small figurines, etc.

Perhaps some of this will appear as though the present writers, too, have soured on everything that is urban Victorian. Not so, by any means. They indeed count themselves among its most ardent admirers, but that admiration has never been allowed to reach the stage of worship. Granted that the Early and Mid-Victorian rooms were more than a bit stuffy, crowded, and with far too much ornamentation and bric-a-brac, this admission is not meant to condemn all of it. Such rooms had their share of charming pieces, homey, comfortable, and in good taste. The problem of the modern collector is that of reassembling such rooms from a modern viewpoint and of avoiding the mistakes of the Victorians in overdoing things. The task is one of achieving a well-thought-out simplification, so as to produce the Victorian effect but without the overcrowding and the ostentatious quality due to the silly foibles of Early Victorian housewives and their efforts to achieve impressive results. Stripped of perhaps as much as one-half of their more gaudy articles, such rooms may be made to present an air of good taste, comfort, and cheer especially when by a careful choice in modern fabrics the overpowering heaviness of the Victorian room is lightened. In this one loses perfect authenticity, to be sure, but then one has to compromise between the purely authentic and the practical aspect of things. After all, the average collector need not try to achieve the technical perfection of the museum.

So much for the moods, vogues, and accomplishments of Early Victorian Americana as it related to the middle-class, upper-middle-class and upper-class homes of this country.

What confuses the beginner more than anything else is the belief that Victorian furniture represents a definite single style. It does nothing of the sort. The word simply refers to a period—a very long period—when anything by way of design could and often did happen. As an example, the period embraced in order of their appearances such almost unrelated styles as a revival of Louis XV, Late Empire, John Hall's massive forms, Belter's overly done pierced carvings, the catastrophe of Charles Eastlake's Medieval Gothic, monstrosities with Turkish inspiration, what briefly became known as U. S. Grant, and, to cap it all, just before the good Queen died the beginning of the vogue for mission furniture. There is, then, no such thing as Victorian furniture; only furniture that was made during the Queen's reign.

For convenience as reference: the period is divided into three parts, Early Victorian (1837–55), Mid-Victorian (1855–70) and Late Victorian (1870–1901). Both good sense from an investment point of view and good taste from an artistic point of view eliminate the Late Victorian and leave only the Early and Mid-Victorian periods from which to choose, at least as to furniture. That which remains after 1870 will one day gather in the years needed for antiquity, but this will be a most undeserved recognition from any viewpoint but a chronological one.

The Late Victorian era followed the year 1870 and brought with it the final corruption. A new ugliness arrived and it was due in a very large measure to one man and the advent of power-driven wood-carving machinery. Large companies with fabulous new means for production at hand were impatient to find new and larger markets, and to do this they had to catch the public fancy. Hence the almost frantic and hysterical experimentation with styles that set in about 1870, and the complete passing of ottomans, box sofas, divans, French bedsteads, three-quarter chairs, and many other fixtures of the Early Victorian era. Came folding beds in Gothic style, Grecian toilet sets in black walnut, elaborate sideboards, "Patent furniture," Witts Patent rockers, Modern Gothic, and above all—the final blow indeed—Charles Eastlake and his monstrous Medieval Gothic.

Eastlake was an officer in the British Institute of Architects and he apparently fancied himself somewhat of an authority on furniture design and home furnishing in general. In 1866 his book, *Hints on Household Taste in Furniture Upholstery, and Other Details,* appeared in England, complete with inserted samples of colored wallpaper. The treatise reached this country in considerable numbers and was widely read, especially by the furniture trade, now hopelessly bankrupt from an artistic point of view and ready and willing to try anything. The manufacturers began to turn to East-

FIG. 7. (Lower) Two ugly, Late Victorian chairs made by Hale and Kilbourne in Philadelphia about 1875. (Upper) A Late (1875) Victorian bed of the folding sort but, artistically speaking, representative of all Late Victorian beds.

lake for inspiration and soon the newly conceived ugliness came into vogue. The vogue reached the proportions of a stampede after a Boston publisher distributed an American edition of Eastlake in 1873.

The American version of Eastlake's bad taste held the center of the stage well into the 1880's. This brought final wreck and ruin to the Victorian era, and for all practical purposes (and for the collector) it may be assumed that this era ended in 1870. The attics and barns of the United States are still loaded with Eastlake's misshapen, ugly things. Here and there we find it coming to market in the shops and one day we shall find that Early and Mid-Victorian things will become so scarce that an Eastlake revival will be carefully fostered by the antique trade.

Here and there during the reign of Charles Eastlake a few things not exactly in Eastlake style did manage to come to market. For one thing there was the so-called cottage furniture. There were little painted chests and commodes, with gay colors and painted floral designs or scenes on the drawer fronts. Although highly decorated they have a certain charm and quaintness that makes them quite acceptable. We still come across them occasionally but there are precious few that are well enough preserved—that is, the paintings —to come within the range of decent restoration. Usually, however, these little chests are clear pine underneath, and for those who like this wood with a clear shellac finish they are good purchases for five dollars.

Such in a nutshell is the machine-versus-hand history of the Early, Mid-Victorian, and Late Victorian periods. If the Victorians created anything worthy of survival, it was produced during the earlier years. Of course, the word Victorian is not to be found in the nomenclature of antiquity as it is recognized by the haughty connoisseurs. Antiquity as it is recognized in orthodox circles leaves off about 1830 or shortly before Duncan Phyfe, the last of the great cabinetmakers, joined the ghosts of Goddard, Townsend, Savery, et al.

It is to be expected that the stuffed shirts of the antique trade will have none of this Victorian business, either early or late, and that they will hold that the whole era produced nothing of value, nothing worth the effort of preservation. That attitude, these writers feel, is far too harsh and is more apt to be the view of a person with a hundred thousand dollar inventory of eighteenth century stuff than to be the mature and honest opinion of one with less cause for prejudice.

What one might call the eighteenth century cult also has its monstrous pets. The Greek revival did not have the monopoly on beauty which its presentday admirers claim for it. Its sins were perhaps not as numerous as those committed by the Victorians but they were sins nevertheless, and many things of the eighteenth century that today pass for examples of sheer beauty are placed in that category by unreasoning veneration more than anything else. To some, the early cabinetmakers and disciples of Chippendale, Hepplewhite, Sheraton, and the brothers Adam could do no wrong; they were purists all working under the sole guidance of heaven. Perhaps one may attribute this in part to the natural adoration in which most humans indulge where antiquity is concerned. All of us have a tendency to venerate things solely because they are old. Doubtless as the Victorian era recedes into a more distant antiquity it, too, will have its share of unreasoning devotees. It has indeed in some measure already passed into the initial phase of such a state. Time was, and not more than a bare twenty-five years ago, when even the choicest of the early Victorian lady's or gentleman's chairs brought only a dollar or two each and that merely because of their purely utilitarian value. Today the same chairs may bring between $75 and $150, depending upon upholstery, mechanical condition, design, wood, and the part of the country in which they are put up for sale. The smarter shops in the eastern urban centers have been known to ask as much as $250 for bare frames of choice types. To the adherents of the eighteenth century cult, however, such chairs amount only to slightly glorified junk unworthy of cartage except perhaps for purely commercial reasons. True, such pieces do not represent the finer subtleties of design any more than do the inspirations responsible for them: the wiry, curvy chairs of Louis XV. Yet the connoisseurs will fall into fits of ecstasy at the mere mention of the early forerunners.

Such are some of the inconsistencies of the antique business. The authors may be pitied for their ignorant blasphemy, but they fail, as do many other honest hobbyists, to find in many of the eighteenth century pieces the exquisite design which these are supposed to have. Exquisite, patient, and flawless workmanship, yes; bonnet tops, spindly cabriole legs supporting a bulky body, no. By way of examples of fine carvings, the Philadelphia school had much to offer. As for their being true works of art, one is certainly on more debatable ground. Rococo in wood is no more admirable in its overdone forms than it is in alabaster. After all, this partiality to eighteenth century work is largely a phenomenon of the last forty years. Before that, only a few desired it. Indeed at the turn of the century, it had been all but forgotten. Those were the days when a presentable highboy or a Hepplewhite sideboard could be knocked down for a few dollars at any New England auction. Today the big city dealer is at the auction with his expert and a bankroll that would clog a sewer.

The things used by lesser people during early Victorian times were quite different. All who write about the early Victorians deal only with the urbanites and the furnishings enjoyed by the wealthy sophisticates of the day. The poor, both provincial and urban, fared differently. The Victorian era was by no means without its primitives wrought by the hands of the humble joiners, carpenters, and home mechanics in the hinterlands. These fellows labored in their small shops to produce strictly utilitarian articles (usually in pine) in the form of dough trays (many of which, by the way, are not nearly as old as most of our antique dealers would have us believe they are), corner cupboards, dry sinks, kitchen tables, hutch tables (in New England), and quaint chairs of hickory and oak. Most Early Victorian farmers were far removed from the fancy furniture shops and, except perhaps for the parlor, depended almost wholly upon the local joiner, the more elaborately equipped of whom boasted a foot-power lathe with which to turn the posts of maple beds and the legs of tables done usually in the walnut or cherry from the farmstead ordering them.

The Victorian era began at a time when hundreds of thousands of eastern residents of the country were moving westward, literally pouring into the regions of the Great Lakes and the valleys of the Ohio and Mississippi rivers. During the 1840's at least half of the farmers in these areas were still living in improved or unimproved log cabins and either making their own crude furniture during the cold winter months or, if a good harvest supplied the funds, ordering pieces from the nearby village joiner. Such articles were solidly and honestly made and most of them that have come down to us have taken their century or more of beating with dignity. They are still in many instances found in service: tables in the milk house bearing pails or in the cellar loaded with canned fruit. Hickory chairs are still to be found in barn lofts or on porches and pine corner cupboards may harbor a hoard of Mr. Woolworth's choicest items.

Many are the mistakes that are made in judging the antiquity of the great remaining mass of such furniture, most people being far too liberal in the number of years they pile upon it. Old New England craftsmen as late as the 1840's were still making Windsor chairs very much in the style of those made in the latter part of the eighteenth century, and all used the same tools, the same methods, and the same woods. Legion indeed are the amateur collectors of antiques who have been hoodwinked into purchasing early Victorian primitives at eighteenth century prices. It is known that hutch tables were made in Vermont as late as the 1880's when the last of the old craftsmen who had defied the machine for so many years had their beloved tools—their molding planes, hollow planes, mallets, chisels, whetstones, gimlets, and bits—snatched from them only by death. None among the young was left trained in the craft; none perhaps was courageous enough to accept the challenge of the gluttonous machines that could turn a spindle and smooth a board before one could say Jack Robinson.

Nothing much has ever been said or written about the Victorian home done in primitives, but the materials needed for its faithful reproduction are abundant and at prices within the range of many pocketbooks. It is easy enough to visualize a dining room or a bedroom in this quaint style, almost Shaker in its stark simplicity. There might be a six-legged table with cherry top and leaves, curly maple legs tapered in the Hepplewhite tradition, six little fancy chairs of the Hitchcock type either with their gaily colored stencils or stripped and shellacked, a chest in solid pine with the lingering air of the eighteenth century about it, a clock shelf with a brass-works Jerome clock beginning to tick into its second century, a pine corner cupboard adorned with handmade molding, a legged dough tray for serving, a Currier and Ives of Andrew Jackson or Martha Washington, a few brass candleholders, a Boston rocker, and an oval rag rug, vintage of 1848.

The provincial Victorian bedroom need not be a whit less charming than the dining room of the same era. There is the four-poster bed with a woven coverlet or a handmade quilt over its modern inner spring mattress, a Boston rocker and a fancy chair, a pine chest and a commode, a cherry bedside table in the Hepplewhite manner, a pine wash stand, a rag rug, perhaps a pine blanket chest at the foot of the bed, and a Currier and Ives or two of the correct date or maybe a primitive portrait in oil or a sampler. As for wood: pine, maple, and cherry enjoy the most natural companionship in any primitive room. As to Hepplewhite, of course, these early joiners in the provinces never heard of him, who lived in another world. They tapered the square legs because it was the only decorative device that could be used without a lathe, which most of them did not possess. The plane was all that was needed to make legs of this type.

Such rooms would be authentic Victorian provincial and the cost might, with careful collecting, be as low as one-third of that which an eighteenth century room of the same type would cost. As for authenticity, the Victorian room would be letter-perfect, just as much so as its urban counterpart of Victorian times so carefully assembled by the experts at the Metropolitan Museum in New York City.

How forgotten is the life of the early Victorian farmer! His existence was almost as primitive as the farmers of one hundred years before him. Do we know that many of these early Victorian farmsteads still used soapstone molds in which to cast their pewter spoons and buttons, flailed wheat, made homespun, made soft soap, hunted with muskets, used chopping bowls cut from the burl of trees, cured their ills from the herb garden, and covered their coffins with calico? The blight of the machine had not yet touched them. Apparently the lure of the eighteenth century still remains so strong that the charm of this era has remained smothered in it. One day our antique collectors will discover it and call it by its correct name: Provincial Victorian. Hats off to the pioneers who have already found it and who enjoy to the utmost the many pleasures it has to offer to the collector!

CHAPTER II

Provincial Victorian
and a Guide to Age

FOR many people, a great section of American antiques have remained nameless in so far as style or the period to which they
may be assigned are concerned. Reference is made to the enormous
mass of provincial furniture, tinware, treenware, crockery, pottery,
homespun, paintings, glassware, silverware, and pewter produced
between the years 1830 and the 1880's. Clearly these things belong
to what should be called Provincial Victorian although these terms
are rarely if ever used. The attics, the cellars, the haymows, the
toolsheds and wagonsheds of many pioneer farms of the early and
middle nineteenth century still shelter articles of this nature and as
Victorian collectibles many of them are also choice Americana.
The great mass of primitive articles that have come down to us
intact were produced during Victorian times. Only the better informed dealer or the well-read layman is able properly to recognize
and identify the period to which these primitives belong.

It is most difficult for many people to appreciate the extremely
primitive existence endured by the families that moved westward
during the first quarter of the nineteenth century. The bravest of
the brave set out from the Atlantic Coast states with their oxcarts
at the turn of the century. The less aggressive went after the opening of the New York State Erie Canal and the canals of Ohio and
Pennsylvania. Thus were Illinois, Indiana, Iowa, Ohio, western
Pennsylvania and western New York settled. The lush lands of
the Midwest were virgin and fertile and stood waiting for the
ax and the plow, for the strong hands whose owners were to

re-enact the drama of their forefathers who settled the coastal states from Virginia to Maine. What these people made was honestly and ruggedly made and what they made in the way of furniture was intensely utilitarian, fashioned from oak, hickory, walnut, wild cherry, pine, and maple.

In the 1860's housewives were still pulling beef pies and bread from basement Dutch ovens and using wrought iron peals (like a long handled shovel) for the purpose. Yet where is the amateur collector, nay the dealer in antiques, who will not insist that the peal was wholly an eighteenth century article? Many were the Midwest and New England farmsteads on which, as late as the 1870's grandmothers and even their daughters were still using their flax hatchels, wool cards, flax wheels, wool wheels and three-legged iron hearth skillets while father flailed his wheat on the barn floor or milked into a hickory piggin. Many were the oxyokes that were not stored away in the haymow or wagonshed until the 1880's! Shocking news indeed for those who insist on stamping such things with a date not later than 1825. Most of them still in existence were in all probability made after Lincoln was president.

The Midwest traveler moving along the provincial roads during the 1830's and 1840's only rarely found anything but log cabin farmsteads, many of them with stump patches filled with waving corn. The twenty years between 1845 and 1865 were the years of transition when log cabins began to be replaced by frame houses— but not all of them. Only the more successful of the settlers could indulge in such luxury.

One is amused these days in listening to the chatter of the neo-phytes in the antique shops. An old pierced tin lantern is picked up and admired. "That," volunteers the dealer, who only a year ago may have been a retired bookkeeper or suddenly changed from the shoe to the antique business, "is at least 175 years old. It's called a Paul Revere lantern." It is difficult to convince such people that the village tinsmiths of the 1830's and 1840's made such lanterns in large numbers. Such glassless lanterns were made only for barn chores. True, they were probably used during the last quarter of the eighteenth century but their popularity persisted into the 1850's and by far the larger number of them that have come down to us are of nineteenth century vintage.

Similar misjudgments are often made in the case of the old grease lamps and so-called betty lamps. Almost without exception they are assigned to Colonial or even Puritan times. Although such lamps were indeed used during early Colonial times, they were also used in the rural districts of Victorian America and perhaps as late as the 1850's and 1860's. The candle, too, along with the candle mold, persisted for many years after the death ascribed to it by amateur antiquarians. What many fail to do is properly to estimate the survival time of many of the articles used by American families.

Many members of the Masonic orders and other lodges carried their little foot warmers to meetings up to a time long after Abraham Lincoln was president of the U.S.A. Grandma then still had her herb garden and here and there in the hinterlands an infusion of whisky and gunpowder was still given to ward off attacks of the ague. For many years after lucifer matches came into use in the early 1840's, backwoodsmen who could not afford such new fangled luxuries had to scotch a flint to kindle a fire and it was many years after this that the farmer could afford to lay away his old flintlock fowling piece and purchase one of the new percussion cap rifles.

The change in American provincial life did not come precipitately. This is especially true of the methods of doing things, of the arts and crafts. During 1806, Aaron Burr was in England looking at the marvelous new invention; the steam-driven circular saw. Although this type of saw was first introduced into this country a few years afterward, its success was by no means instant. Thirty years were required before such saws found wide usage and then largely in the centers of great population. The saw pit and the gash saw were still used in the 1840's and the frame saws were used in hydraulic sawmills for many years after the circular saw was an accepted thing. As a matter of record, the last of the water-power mills was not dismantled until 1902. It had been driven by the waters of Roaring Run Creek in Huntington County, Pennsylvania, since the year 1800.

What the newcomer to collectible antiques fails to realize is that no era or period, no style or custom, no craft or skill or method broke off abruptly. In all instances of change, there is an overlapping period which may cover ten, twenty, or even a hundred years.

And that quaint little hickory rocker with the back slats mortised and pinned into the posts; how old is it? The guesses are apt to cover a wide range. Although rockers in general were very rare prior to 1800 and then made only by conversion of other chairs, many of the uninformed would swear that a chair of the type just mentioned would be of the eighteenth century. Does it not have wooden pegs?

Adherents of what might be called the Wooden Peg cult among the collectors of antiques entertain many amusing misconceptions about early joinery. Anything with pegs in it must "go way back" and consequently must be regarded with reverence. The truth is that all of the provincial Victorian cabinetmakers who assembled what may now be called Victorian primitives used hickory or oak pegs to hold their mortised joints.

How silly the notion that pegs were used because there were no nails! It is known that the Romans made wrought iron nails in exactly the same manner as the New England "nailers" of 1790. Several Roman nail-heading anvils have been dug up in Europe, one of them at Heidelberg and now in a German museum at Speyer.

The early joiners and cabinetmakers of America did not depend too much on nails because of the excellency of their mortised joints, dovetails, etc., all of them much more effective than the free use of the convenient nail would guarantee. Usually the only place where nails were used was in attaching molding and the crude backboards of chests and corner cupboards. In many cases, especially among the more painstaking of the Victorian joiners, this practice held until late in the nineteenth century.

The collecting fraternity includes not only the Wooden Peg cult but also the Old Nail cult. Many assume that any article of

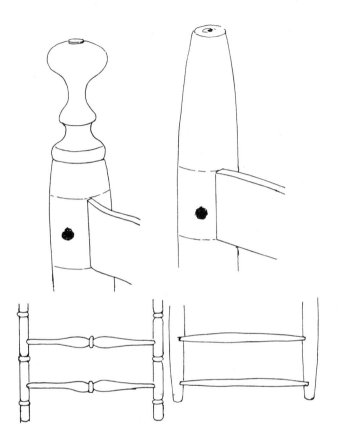

FIG. 8. As an example of the deterioration both in design and workmanship that took place between the last part of the eighteenth century and the early part of the nineteenth century, some of the details on ladder-back or slat-back chairs representing the two centuries are shown above. The left shows the finial, legs and stretchers of a chair made during the 1780's. The right illustrates the stark design of a ladder-back, made in the 1830's; which is minus all decorative turnings.

furniture having in it a few square nails must have been made about the time Noah boarded the ark. That is a tricky and deceptive rule to follow in view of the fact that square nails may still be purchased from any well-stocked lumber yard or hardware store. The Vikings used practically the same sort of nail in shipbuilding. The famous Oseberg ship unearthed in 1903 and built about 835 A.D. was found to be planked with the aid of square nails!

There is a difference between the handmade square nail and the machine-made nail which was introduced in this country about 1800. The machine-produced nail is uniform in size and has a smoother surface. Not so with the handmade nail. This bears the overlapping dents produced by the hammer, and its head is never quite square although it is vastly superior to the machine-made nail.

One would think that the advent of the machine-cut square nail about 1800 would have almost instantly retired the handmade nail from the market. This was not so by any means. The machine-made nail was so brittle that it could not be clenched (bent over) without breaking it. Therefore the nailers and blacksmiths went on making handmade nails although in greatly diminishing quantities until 1870 when metallurgical improvements finally brought a clenchable machine-made nail which is still being produced for special purposes although not in large numbers. The general use of the square nail did not cease until 1890 when the present wire nail was introduced.

But why all of this wordage on pegs and nails? First, to destroy some silly notions about the use of pegs and nails, notions that have misled many amateurs in determining the antiquity of furniture. The nail is not to be trusted as a reliable indicator of age. The same sort of nail might be in an 1850 primitive as is found in a 1750 primitive. The screwnail or simply the woodscrew, as it is called today, can be a more reliable guide to antiquity.

The finding of a screw of any type in a piece of furniture often produces great disappointment for amateur collectors, who believe that the screw is a recent invention. Again, this is not so. It too, is an ancient device. Handmade screws were used as early as 1588

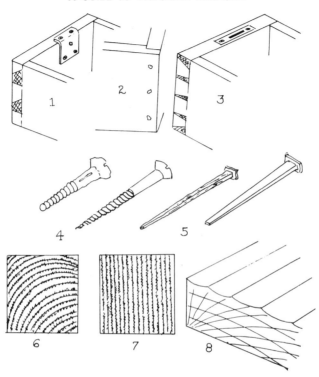

Fig. 9. (1, 2, and 3) Represent methods of drawer construction used during early and Victorian times. (1) Is a drawer front made during the latter part of the eighteenth century with wide dovetail joints and an old iron lock. (2) A nailed and rabbeted drawer front used both during Colonial and Victorian times in somewhat careless construction. (3) A Late Victorian drawer front with narrow, pointed dovetails and a mortised lock. (4 and 5) Show the difference between handmade wood screws used until 1800 and the modern machine-made gimlet screw introduced in 1847. Also shown is an example of the hand-forged square nail made as late as the 1870's, and the machine-cut square nail introduced toward the latter part of the eighteenth century and used with some improvements until the introduction of the wire nail in 1890. (6 and 7) Show the kerf marks left by circular saws and by the old gash, frame, and whip saws. (8) Illustrates the marks left by a hollow plane. The ridges were later scraped off, leaving a telltale undulating surface to distinguish the hand-dressed board from the perfectly flat, machine-dressed board.

32

when the *Machine Book* of the Italian engineer, Ramelli, showed woodscrews being produced with a quaint hand mill. Moxon, too, in his book on *Smithing* published in 1678 mentions them as used to fasten locks to doors.

It is not known definitely when the screwnail was introduced in America but it was used on some very early furniture to replace the clenched nails employed for the installation of hinges on table leaves. We do know that the handmade screw was used up to the first few years of the nineteenth century. One cannot be too sure of the date on any handmade screw. Certainly it is not safe to use such screws as an index of age except in a general way. It was far too early to have been used on even the earliest of the Victorian primitives. Unlike the appearance of the machine-cut square nail, which did not wholly replace the hand-forged square nail until the 1870's, the first of the machine-cut screws must quickly have replaced the hand-made article for reasons of much lower cost and the advantage of one type over the other. The machine-produced product was definitely superior in every way and cost much less.

This introduction of the machine-cut screw took place some time between the close of the eighteenth century and the first few years of the nineteenth. Here the overlapping period must have been very short. The joiners of the day could not afford to keep a large stock of expensive handmade screws on hand. Therefore the discovery of any article of furniture bearing handmade screws may be accepted as fairly reliable evidence of a life that began prior to 1810.

Handmade wood screws may be discovered easily by their crudeness. They are to be found almost exclusively in hand-wrought hinges on blanket chest lids, corner cupboard doors, and the like. They were only rarely used for other purposes, certainly not for the general purposes of fabrication. Even when removed from the same hinge such screws are rarely if ever of the same length. Some are short, some may be relatively long. Examination with a glass will reveal file marks and usually the jaw marks of the vise in which they were held while being worked upon. These appear in the shank of the screw. The slot for the screw driver was either filed or sawed and was rarely across the exact center of the head of the screw. Also such screws had blunt instead of pointed ends. Thus they had to be started in a gimlet hole of the correct diameter.

Machine-made wood screws had blunt ends until 1847 when the present gimlet or pointed screw was introduced. However one should not accept the discovery of a machine-made blunt-end screw as definite evidence that the piece of furniture from which it came was made prior to 1847. Machine-made blunt-end screws were relatively cheap, and the joiners of the day usually had a large supply on hand. This supply might have lasted them for a number of years. Hardware stores, too, kept such screws for a number of years after the introduction of the new type of screw. However, when a sharp-pointed screw (it was first called a gimlet screw) is removed from a hinge or other spot in a piece of furniture and there is no evidence of its having been used to replace an older type of screw, one may with safety place the date of the piece after 1850.

A few more words concerning the use of the wooden peg might prove helpful. This is an extremely early device but it is also a very late device. Grand Rapids uses it to this very day. However, the pegs of old were not the round, smooth, machine-cut things that they are today. They were usually of oak, hickory, or ash, crudely cut and never really round. As a matter of fact, many of them were almost square. The presence of a truly round peg in a piece of furniture of primitive design should make one rather suspicious of the vintage of the piece.

Pegs were of all sizes ranging from the diameter of a match to the diameter of a broomstick or even larger where the pinning of barn and house timbers was concerned. Sometimes they were smeared with animal glue before they were inserted but more often without it, especially in the earlier times. In some of the earlier and larger types of pegs the wedge is found associated with them—a wedge and a peg in the same hole. This was an ingenious arrangement whereby the end of the wedge was expanded as it was driven into the hole in the wood.

Early American primitives of Puritan times and those from the early part of the first half of the eighteenth century were often unpainted. During the second half of the eighteenth century and well on toward the middle of the nineteenth century a great deal of the primitive furniture was painted with a crude mixture of what was known as "earth colors" and a concoction of sour milk, the formula varying perhaps with the various joiners or farmers who used the mixture. Chemically speaking, the use of milk is not difficult to understand. Here was the forerunner of the modern wall coverings in the water-paint family, all of them with a casein base. Casein happens to be richly supplied in milk and it also happens to be a rather stable chemical compound.

The early colors were few. One had to choose between red, green, gray, and, less frequently, white. On one or two occasions joiners' bills have been found wherein a charge was made for Windsor chairs painted white although, until a few years ago, most authorities would have argued the point.

Beginning in 1815 and perhaps as late as 1850, but more especially during the earlier part of the nineteenth century, what became known as the "mahoganized finish" was used. This might have been called "poor man's mahogany" and the finish was usually applied on pine. It was especially popular on tall clock cases of pine that were made locally to house the wooden clock works sold by Silas Hoadley, Riley Whiting, *et al.*, the mahogany effect being produced by a deep red paint, carefully and often ingeniously smeared with streaks of black to simulate the more costly wood.

At this point it might be well to mention that one has a right to be suspicious of lately applied coats of white paint especially in cases where a sizable amount of money is asked for an article of old furniture. This simple method has often been used by the shysters of the antique trade to hide heavy restoration.

Naturally when the more formal and urban furniture made during Early or Mid-Victorian times is to be examined for age, the rules that may be applied to primitive pieces do not apply. Here one must be guided more by style, drawer pulls, the later methods used in construction, etc.

If any article of furniture comes to the collector complete with its original hardware or with only a piece or two of it, this too may serve as a reliable guide to age. It is quite true that excellent reproductions both of wrought-iron hinges and of the earlier types of drawer brasses are being legitimately made and used today, but when such things are employed to replace originals one expects a dealer to be honest enough to volunteer the information. So far as

FIG. 10. Early Victorian and Pre-Victorian glass-knob drawer pulls. (1) Cut glass with glass screw threads invented and patented by Deming Jarves of the Sandwich Glass Company in 1826. This was also made with pressed-glass designs similar to No. 3. (2) Pressed-glass swirl pattern with hole in center and provided with machine screw. (3) The conventional type of pressed-glass knob widely used on furniture between 1830 and 1845 and appearing both in clear flint and opalescent glass. All three knobs were used during these years.

these writers know, no reproductions of Victorian brasses have been made up to the present time, although in a few cases carved-leaf chest pulls of the Late Victorian type have been advertised.

One cannot easily say when the ordinary round-knob chest pull of wood was introduced save to maintain that it made its appearance in this country during very early times. It was used throughout all of the nineteenth century and is in fact still in use.

At one time during the late 1860's and up to the 1880's the popularity of the round wooden knob was challenged by the introduction of the wooden carved-leaf drawer pull. Since the latter was more decorative its public acceptance was great and the innovation went hand in hand with the various other monstrosities of the East-lake period. This was during the time when the furniture-makers used a great deal of chestnut in making the cheaper types of bed-room furniture.

Many, too, were the glass knobs used during the whole of the Victorian period, many of them pressed by Sandwich. A few of the early ones used on expensive furniture were of cut glass. Occa-sionally one finds fine examples of the plain cut-glass knob on the heavily carved mahogany pieces of Late Empire.

Pressed-glass knobs came in three sizes: large, medium, and small, the latter being used on the bedside stands and the smaller articles of furniture. Some were of clear and some of opalescent glass, and both the late and early types were fastened with machine screws, the female member or nut of the screw being imbedded in the glass and made to stick by means of molten lead.

The most desirable knobs of this nature were used before 1850 and when unbroken they add distinct value to any article of furni-ture upon which they were used. Depending on type, they may range from $2.50 to $5.00 in price. The opalescent knobs are by far the most valuable. Especially desirable are the pressed-glass knobs invented, patented (1829), and marketed by Deming Jarves during the early 1830's. Jarves, it will be recalled, was the founder of the Sandwich Glass Company. This knob is all glass, requiring no metal for attachment and being pressed with a screw shank. This screw shank was threaded directly into the drawer upon which the knob was used.

Not all of the early pressed knobs were "fancy." Some were plain, some bore only ribbing, and a few were cut with diamond motifs, the latter being rather rare, however.

The white porcelain knob was also used, especially during the 1850's and 1860's, but it was a cheap affair purchased for a few pennies at any village hardware store. It was used on furniture as a substitute, and then only by careless families without pride. It was really intended for kitchen cupboards, drawers, jelly cupboards, and the like and is therefore usually found only on primitive furniture.

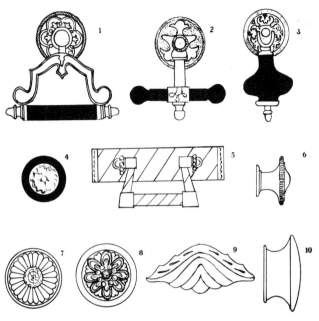

FIG. 11. Drawer pulls used between 1840 and 1890. (1, 2, and 3) Were popular between 1870 and 1885. (4) Brass and wood of Civil War period. (5) Late 1880's. (6) All brass, late 1840's and 1850's. (7) All brass. Used throughout 1840's and 1850's. (8) Pressed glass. Used in various patterns during 1830-1860. (9) Carved drawer pull of 1870's and 1880's. Various patterns, all with nature motifs, were used. (10) Turned wooden knob used from earliest times to present day.

During the late 1870's the better grades of furniture appeared with fancy metal pulls. A number of these took the teardrop form used on the William and Mary styles of early times. Some drops were all metal, some of turned wood with a metal rod for a center which was swivelled at its upper end. It was also during this time that the drop pull with a cross member appeared.

Apparently the early bail handle, so popular in the baroque styles of chest and highboy hardware during the latter part of the eighteenth century, was not reintroduced to any great extent until the 1890's. Certainly the bail handles were not popular either during the Early or Mid-Victorian periods.

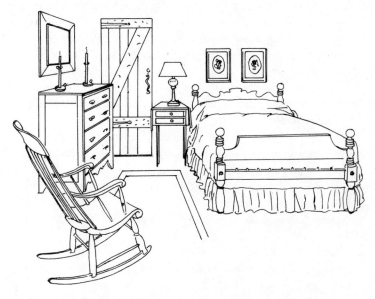

Fig. 12. A Provincial Victorian bedroom which may be in maple or cherry or a combination of both. Chests similar to the one shown may be had in maple, cherry, or pine. The latter wood was not often used for beds because it lacked strength.

Occasionally the collector of Victorian antiques will come across odd pieces of drawer-pull hardware not identifiable with the American scene. If it is of rococo style and the chest or other article of furniture upon which it is found is difficult to place in relation to the American scene, the chances are that it is French and probably imported into this country before the days of the protective tariff. Not a small amount of such furniture came into the larger of the urban centers of America during the 1850's.

So much for knobs and drawer pulls in glass, metal, and wood as they tell the story of period. Here and there the collector will come upon hardware that does not appear in these classifications and styles, but the occasion will be rare. In general it will be found that the foregoing discourse on the subject will supply the casual collector with reliable guidance to date. However, no definite date can be ascribed to any piece bearing such devices as those described because of that bugaboo, overlapping use. Here and there items can be nailed down to a definite year, but only rarely. However, there is no need for such accuracy. Any collector should be satisfied in the knowledge that he may date his or her possessions within a three to five year bracket, and somebody in the nature of a clairvoyant is required to do better than that.

Returning to the subject of provincial furniture produced during the first half of the nineteenth century or even between the years 1800 to 1870: the reader is warned against taking a dogmatic position where questions of age are concerned. Only here and there during these times was there any set style in vogue. Indeed even the urban furniture made between the years 1800 and 1840 was in a sad state of confusion with a number of vogues seeking public approval simultaneously. Thus the first years of the nineteenth century saw the almost complete fading of Chippendale, the passing of the brief period of French Directoire, the late twilight of Hepplewhite and Sheraton, the introduction of Napoleon's Empire and the early or first stage of American Empire, etc. Later came English Regency (although it had little influence in America except in chairs and was itself borrowed largely from French Directoire) and the later, heavier form of American Empire. All were influenced by the neo-classic trend that had begun during the last half of the previous century.

In so far as urban or formal furniture is concerned, the first thirty-five years of the nineteenth century are very difficult to master, furniture-wise. During the first twenty years, Americans were attempting to give much of their furniture a touch of patriotic feeling, which brings in the term American Federal. Federal touches were largely decorative rather than involving any basic changes in design. For instance, there was the round, convex mirror with gold frame and a spread eagle adorning its top; brass eagle door knockers; eagle, beehive, or crossed-cannon bail pulls for chests, etc.

However, the country cabinetmaker or the farmer working in his shed or beside his winter hearth was little influenced by these trends, and there is little difference in the primitive furniture produced between 1790 and 1815, but gradually the great charm fathered by the eighteenth century people (provincial) began to wear off. There were fewer and fewer Windsor chairs with nicely proportioned thick saddle seats, delicately tapered spindles, delicate bows, or prettily turned stretchers or rungs. The Windsors became cruder and cruder, as did the ladder- or slat-backs with their back slats reduced in number until three finally came to be almost standard. Nor did many of the later makers bother to scroll the tops of slats or to give them the thinness or sweeping lateral curve that they once had.

While country chests in pine, cherry, and maple continued to be made with Chippendale bracket feet minus the cyma recta or ogee curve, the scrolls lost their eighteenth century charm and the workmanship in general began to deteriorate. The country had for the first time lost its leisurely viewpoint. People began to be in a hurry to get things done.

Some collectors of primitive furniture rely upon the saw marks left in wood for a guide to age. The back boards of many early chests, corner cupboards, and the like were left unfinished just as they came from the saw. Thus it has been thought that the kerf marks left by the saw may serve to date a piece of furniture as being early or late. The pit saw or whipsaw and the gash saw of the early water power sawmills, with their up and down motion, left parallel kerf marks, a saw stroke apart. On the other hand, the circular saw left a series of semi-circular kerf marks as boards moved into them.

This method of calculating age can be very deceptive although the writers once subscribed to it. It so happens that the circular saw

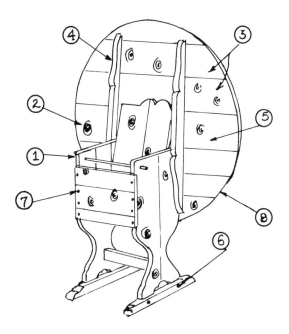

Fig. 13. Reproductions of old pine primitives may easily be detected if the following points are covered: (1) Standard dimensional pine lumber comes in two thicknesses only; ⅛ and ¾ inch. Either one of these dimensions on boards is a dead giveaway. Old cabinetmakers usually used boards one inch or more in thickness. (2) Knowing the modern ladies' weakness for knotty pine, all of the shysters try to accommodate them. It is usually difficult to find a single knot in an old pine piece. (3) Table tops, chest ends and tops, etc., were in the old days made of the widest possible boards, often with a width of eighteen inches or more. Too many boards in a top is a bad sign. (4) One should also watch out for modern pine 2 x 4's which actually measure 1⅞ x 3¾ inches. (5) A smooth machine-produced surface on boards can be detected by your laying a straight edge across them. (6) Perfectly round wooden pegs were never used. (7) Purchasers should watch for puttied nail heads, indicative of trickery. (8) Look out for artificial wear on edges with wood rasp.

was not adapted to operation by water wheels. The circular saw required speed for efficient operation. Hence a complicated and expensive system of pulleys and belts had to be installed with water wheels, and few indeed were the poor owners of mills who could afford such newfangled contraptions. They stuck to their old frame saws for many years after the introduction of the circular saw from England some time after 1810. The circular saw had to await the introduction of the steam engine and it was not until the late 1840's that such saws came into wide use. This is not to say that they were not used here and there between 1815 and 1850. Up to 1850 and in many cases many years beyond this, the crude old sawmills of the frame saw type, limped along to supply the country with timber and boards.

Saw kerf marks are therefore of limited importance as an index of antiquity. However, if one is asked to purchase a pine corner cupboard supposedly from the eighteenth century and the back boards of that cupboard have rotary saw kerf marks, the invitation to purchase should be politely declined. Many were the pine cupboards produced after the circular saw was in wide use and many of these cupboards possess the simple charm of much earlier furniture. It is rare indeed to find a piece of furniture made before 1825 that bears the marks of the circular saw except perhaps in those communities that boasted of one of the early steam sawmills.

For some unaccountable reason the passing years brought about a change in the size of the dovetails used in the making of chest drawers and this holds both for formal and for primitive. Before the year 1800, such dovetails were larger although not as large as they were during and before the first half of the eighteenth century. Between the 1800's and 1840's, these dovetails became quite small, more of them being used. On the whole, it is fairly safe to assume that a chest with small dovetails in the drawers was not made prior to 1825 or thereabouts. This is simply a general rule.

Many years passed before one could go to a lumber yard as we do today and purchase accurately dressed boards. Doubtless during the middle part of the nineteenth century cabinetmakers in the rural districts could go to a mill and purchase roughed-out boards and timbers, but the actual dressing (smoothing) of such lumber was something that had to be done in the small shop and by the use of hand planes. For this work the so-called hollow plane was employed, a plane with the cutting edge of the blade slightly rounded to overcome the digging in of its corners. This blade left a slightly wavy or undulated surface, the slight ridges being removed later by the use of a scraper. Boards prepared and dressed in this manner are easily detected. If one will gently sweep one's fingers across a board that was dressed in the manner just described, one can feel the slight undulations in the surface. The evidence offered, however, is certainly not to be accepted as conclusive proof of great antiquity. Many old provincial cabinetmakers were still dressing their boards in this manner as late as 1860 or later.

Such examination can be useful at times, however. If a certain piece of primitive furniture is being offered to a collector as being very old and the test proves it was made of machine-finished boards, the evidence is conclusive that the article is not old; only old enough perhaps for the pine or other wood to have taken on the discoloration that comes with age. Even fifty or sixty years will deepen the color of any wood. Not enough to fool the expert perhaps, but certainly enough to hoodwink the beginner. The surface test will also disclose the presence of reproductions.

Reproductions, however, are not nearly so plentiful as one might think, especially in these days of high labor costs. Old-furniture fakes do not pay unless they imitate great rarities or fast-selling articles that can be easily reproduced by machinery. There would be a handsome profit in producing early butterfly and gate-leg tables of an eighteenth century design if one could be continuously successful with the deception. Eighteenth century Windsor chair frauds could also be profitable because of the high prices that the originals demand.

There is no doubt that some eighteenth century corner cupboards, hutch tables, and the like have been reproduced and sold as originals during the past few years, a few of them reaching the hands of honest dealers who unwittingly sold them for what they thought them to be. During the preparation of this book one of these writers saw such a hutch table in the sales room of a dealer who was known to be scrupulously honest although not too cognizant of the telltale marks of furniture humbuggery. The table in question invited careful inspection because of its overemphasized crudities. For one thing, its pine boards had too many knots. Old cabinetmakers avoided knots as far as possible. Perfectly round pegs were also used and every board was as smooth as a mirror. The "worn" edges were obviously produced with a wood rasp. Who among dishonest tinkers would not make such a simple table if he could sell it to an antique dealer for one hundred dollars?

The very popular Victorian six-legged drop-leaf table in maple, cherry, walnut, and mahogany has been reproduced no end during the past few years. These tables bring as much as $275 and, if one can get away with it, may be very profitably reproduced and sold as antiques. In the writers' own territory some four hundred such tables were released into the channels of the antique trade during the single year of 1947. A small western New York furniture manufacturer happened to purchase a large supply of old cherry and walnut wood and he could not resist the temptation to transform it into the popular Mid-Victorian drop-leaf tables. With modern machine methods, such tables may be made for twenty dollars or less and they will bring $150 or more in the antique shops. The manufacturer in question sold all of his tables to a few shyster dealers who quickly netted a $100 profit on each one.

Such trickery is still going on in various parts of the country and it is a shame, too, because of the ease with which such work can be detected if one will but demand that the "thoroughly reconditioned" table (as the crooked dealer will probably maintain) be turned upside down. There is not, however, any chance of detecting such fakes by looking for old tool marks and the like, for the methods used in producing the original tables of this type were practically the same as the methods used in making furniture today. If upon such inspection underneath a table it is found that all of the boards of the table frame are fresh and new, some explanation should be forthcoming as such boards in truly old tables are dark even though the table top has been refinished.

The old cabinetmaker who could boast of a "turner's bench" or lathe and who made ladder or slat-back chairs, four poster beds, and the like usually left telltale marks on their turned articles of wood. The marks left by the turning tool are often visible under the right kind of light. The early turning lathes were turned slowly, usually by a "great wheel" and belt, the wheel being turned by means of a crank and a hard-working apprentice. Few indeed were the old craftsmen who, like Eli Terry at Plymouth, Connecticut, could set up lathes driven by water power. Power-driven, modern lathes turning at two thousand revolutions per minute or better never leave a tool mark nor did the steam driven lathes of early or mid-Victorian times.

Old ladder-back chair posts will usually be found with scriber or awl marks left on them at the points where the slats are mortised in. While the posts were still in the lathe after being turned, the worker touched them (they were still revolving) with the sharp point of the awl and at the section between which the mortises for the slats were to be cut. Such workers rarely bothered to remove these layout marks later.

The vogue for fancy painted furniture or provincial type lasted for many years and it is often difficult to assign certain pieces of such furniture to a definite date without allowing for a five-year inaccuracy one way or the other. Many collectors also think that Hitchcock was the pioneer of painted chairs and painted furniture. The truth is that in the nineteenth century the Adam brothers, Robert and James, at one time had in their employ in England such renowned painters as Pergolesi and Cipriani so that their furniture would surely be acceptable to the English aristocracy.

The present writers do not know who started the vogue for painted furniture here in America during the early part of the nineteenth century. It is conceded that Lambert Hitchcock at least gave a great deal of emphasis to the craze with his "fancy chairs," decorated for the trade with stencils.

Fancy stencilled furniture was very popular between the years 1825 and 1845, offering as it did a degree of elegance for people who had the desire for hand-painted furniture but lacked the pocketbook. Nor was such decoration limited to chairs. One occasionally comes upon a stencilled chest or stencilled four-poster bed made between the years mentioned above, although they are scarce. The writers have in their collection such a bed with the baluster and headpiece stencilled with a Masonic motif. Clocks with such decorations on their pilasters are much more common, and practically all of them were equipped with wooden works made either by Silas Hoadley, Eli Terry, Riley Whiting, or Chauncey Jerome.

Chest and cabinet locks, too, may help one to determine age within rough limits. The early and midcentury locks of the nineteenth century are of the primitive iron type shown in one of the accompanying illustrations. They rested in a crudely cut recess in the back of the drawer front. Such locks persisted up to and beyond the Civil War. Later locks were mortised into the drawer fronts. For the layman, however, there is little to distinguish between a lock installed in 1835 and in 1855. The discovery of such things can very well assure one that a chest was perhaps made before 1865 or thereabouts.

Much of the iron hardware produced between 1800 and 1840 was from the village forge although brass manufactured hinges, draw pulls, locks, latches, casters, etc., were imported from England during the very early part of the nineteenth century. Small iron hinges for tables were also made in this country during these times and in so far as the casual collector is concerned, such hinges are much the same as those produced at the present time.

Although most eighteenth century vogues were cast off during the first few years of the nineteenth century, some lingered on for many years. Eli Terry popularized the pillar and scroll clock case designed by Heman Clark and this had a swan neck scroll for its cornice. By 1800, Chippendale was a faded favorite but his scrolled bracket feet lingered on, usually in unmolded form. Such feet are indeed used to this very day. One may find Chippendale on a country pine chest of the 1830's, on a mahogany chest of the 1840's or 1940's.

Hepplewhite, too had a slow nineteenth century death, if indeed he is wholly dead even today. Many of the old cabinetmakers during the first half of the nineteenth century, most of whom never had heard of the gentleman who had become so much of a vogue during the last quarter of the eighteenth century, used the tapered leg so much favored by Hepplewhite but by no means original with him. The tapered leg on tables was a simple form of decoration that could be produced with a saw and a plane. It is somewhat amusing to find people who should know better referring to crude bedside candlestands and drop-leaf tables with tapered square legs as being Hepplewhite.

It must be clear, then, that even for the expert, the business of assigning definite dates to the primitives produced during the early part of the nineteenth century is pretty much of a guessing game if one wishes to be honest about it. But is it not enough to know that a certain article is old, without insisting upon definite dates? This might indeed be the case if so many of the newly arrived "dealers" did not use age as an index to selling prices: the older the thing is, the more it will bring. This is apparently the rule. Hence all guesses are made on the safe side which accounts for the one hundred-year errors so frequently made in the trade. Honest dealers will agree only that a certain article of the nineteenth century is old unless it has some distinguishing mark by which it may be more accurately dated. The present writers have more than once been offered articles "at least 150 years old" that were as Victorian as the lace on the Queen's petticoats.

CHAPTER III

Victorian and Early
Nineteenth Century Chairs

COUNTLESS early and mid-nineteenth century chairs have come down to us, many of them in an excellent state of preservation which speaks well for the type of patient workmanship of the early craftsman. What a pity that this type of workmanship did not persist much beyond 1850 but gave way to the scourge of the machine!

Many still are the quaint little hickory, ash, maple, and oak chairs that are hauled down from barn loft rafters and farm attics, seatless and web-covered, but still with a certain dignity and indeed a certain defiance of time and the years. One wonders how long the American chairs being made today will last, with their machine-cut parts, plastic adhesives, and mass assembly. This much may be said: most of them will be used for firewood long before the last of the early nineteenth century veterans have given up the ghost!

From 1820 to 1845 chairs of all types intended for the provincial trade were both mass made and individually produced. Although many of all types have survived the years, the best by far are those that were produced by hand in all probability by hinterland craftsmen: a tinkering farmer working before the winter hearth or a recognized member of the Chairmakers' Guild, forerunner of the present crafts unions.

Chairs are rather easily recognized as being handmade or factory-made after a little experience in comparing provincial chairs of this era. For instance the back posts of the ladder-back chairs of this time invariably had scriber marks at the point where the slat (a chair slat, as in the ladder-back, is horizontal; a splat is a scrolled vertical back board) was mortised into the post. The purpose was to guide the workman in cutting the mortise to the proper length. In the case of mass-produced chairs, such marks were eliminated before the chairs left the factory.

Some tinkers used oak or hickory pegs about one-eighth inch in

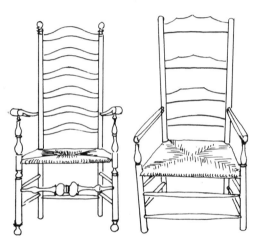

FIG. 14. (Left) A Pennsylvania type ladder or slat back chair made in the last half of the eighteenth century. (Right) The crude slat backs made during the 1830's and 40's.

diameter to keep the ends of slats from working free of the mortise. (See drawing Chapter II) A chair, thought to belong to the first half of the nineteenth century, which does not have these pegs should not be assumed to be of a later period. The use of pegs in the country-made chair was not universal. In all probability it was used more by the tinker than by the professional joiner because the tinker was less sure of the tightness of his mortise.

Especially easy to detect are the armed rockers, produced by the grandfathers, village joiners, and other erstwhile tinkers. The mass-produced rockers and chairs, to be more fully discussed later, were pretty slick from the standpoint of surface finish. No marks of the scraper, the plane, the jackknife, or the draw knife is to be found on these articles. Not so with the country-made stuff. Even the village joiner, who was not too careful about details of finish, left telltale surface defects, especially in the form of draw knife marks on the stretchers or rungs of chairs. Nor were his rocking chair arms perfectly formed, shaved out as they were by hand. Usually, however, the back posts of the chair were turned by a lathe but this is by no means an invariable rule. Some were carefully worked round with a draw knife.

Unlike the ladder backs and the fine Windsors produced during the eighteenth century, the primitive chairs (rockers, Windsors and ladder backs) belonging to the nineteenth century were usually without the decorative rungs except those made during the first years. This is a general statement. There are exceptions, naturally. The back posts of the eighteenth century ladder backs usually had finials of some sort at the top. The drawings will help the reader to distinguish the characteristics of the nineteenth century as compared to the eighteenth century chair, but let no beginning collector think that the general design of the more decorative eighteenth century article was suddenly abandoned on New Year's Eve, December 31, 1799. Many of the finest types of Windsors were made during the early years of the nineteenth century.

Many of the earlier (eighteenth century, that is) ladder-back chairs had as many as seven slats, rarely less than four. On the other hand, most of those made during the first half of the nineteenth century rarely had more than four slats. Whereas many of the slats of the earlier ladder backs were carefully bowed, thin, and delicately curved or scrolled at the top, the nineteenth century types were usually less curved and less thin, due to haste in construction, no doubt. Indeed, the slats in many of these chairs were really not slats at all but hand-shaved spindles mounted horizontally. These were produced by the aid of a draw knife and a spoke shave, and were whittled out with only a slight contour.

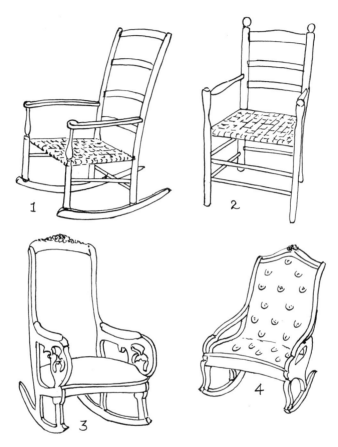

Fig. 15. (1) A Shaker rocker, product of the religious sect of that name and made as an article of commerce by its members during most of the nineteenth century. Such chairs were displayed by the Shakers at the Philadelphia Centennial Exhibition in 1876. (2) A late form of ladder or slat back chair produced in the 1880's. (3) The Lincoln rocker and the (4) so-called slipper rockers, next to the lady's and gentleman's chairs the most popular seats of the Mid-Victorian period.

The expert can trace chairs and other articles of early furniture to their homeland. There is, indeed a geographical significance to antiques. For instance, the Pennsylvania ladder backs and Windsors differed from the New England styles, especially in the design of the turned stretchers and posts. Later on, after the fancy chair was introduced in New England, this, too, gradually developed geographical identification marks.

It is also to be noted that the younger and more hastily made chair of the early nineteenth century practically abandoned the decorative turned leg and rung. Apparently it required too much time, but there is also the fact that but few joiners owned turning lathes. The country was expanding rapidly and many village tinkers jumped into the business of making chairs and other articles of furniture. It was characteristic of the factory-made fancy chairs of the day to have fancy turned legs and front rungs, but this was not so as a general thing in the case of the chair produced in the small shop.

In discussing ladder-back chairs one cannot afford to dismiss the industrious Shaker chair-makers whose handiwork is still to be found about, their chairs having been made for general sale between the years 1825 and 1890. Indeed the Lebanon Pennsylvania Shakers not only exhibited at the Philadelphia Centennial in 1876 but also passed out a booklet describing their wares. The chairs were all ladder backs including rockers and they ranged in price from $3.50 to $8.50 each. During the whole period of their manufacture by the Shakers these chairs were consistently uniform in design and there is very little that the student has to work on in estimating age. They were good chairs, too, structurally speaking.

One should not be too skeptical about the weakness of early primitive chairs when they are found in seatless condition. Usually the rush bottoms of such chairs are either punched out or rotted out and if the chair is worked laterally the frame will be found to wiggle badly. That, however, does not necessarily denote incurable debility. The point to be considered by the prospective purchaser is: are the parts all present and in their proper places, especially the rungs? One will be surprised at the return of the inherent strength of such chairs when a rush bottom is tightly woven in place.

If one does not believe this let him attempt to pull one of the rungs out of the legs. Although these rung ends have been in their holes for anywhere from 100 to 150 years, removal by mere pulling usually defies even the strong man. But why? One finds no evidence of glue (it was the Mid-Victorian furniture factories that began

Fig. 16. Drawn from a Victorian settle of cherry
and known to have been made in the 1840's.

smearing glue about) no pegs, nails, or screws. This uncanny strength was for a long time quite a mystery to the present writers until they found the secret of it while reading some old books devoted to joinery. Usually the posts or legs of such chairs were made of unseasoned maple or other hardwood while the rungs or stretchers were made of seasoned hickory, oak, or ash. As the unseasoned wood dried out, it grasped the ends of the seasoned rungs with a firmness that could not be achieved in any other manner. Only rarely did the cabinetmakers prior to the 1850's make use of large amounts of animal glue.

Although it is thought by many amateur collectors of American antiques that the settle was strictly an eighteenth century seat for use before the hearth, it is known that such things were made and used in the rural sections of this country as late as the 1840's or possibly the 1850's. Most were in pine although here and there one finds one done in cherry, oak, or even walnut.

The reason for the use of pine in furniture requiring large boards is not difficult to understand inasmuch as many craftsmen had to saw and dress their own boards. Pine was plentiful and it was easily worked. Not only that but, when properly seasoned, it warped very little over the years. It is true that its strength was not great but when it was used with good joints in the construction of box or cabinet furniture it was sufficiently strong for all ordinary use. Save for settles, it was not used for chairs, its strength not being sufficient for this purpose.

Returning to the settle, it is noted that on the whole, nineteenth century furniture of this type was less decorative than the eighteenth century pieces. Settles were less apt to be nicely scrolled or to have applied handmade molding. In this they followed the general rule that nineteenth century primitive furniture was apt to be less decorative than that coming from the preceding century.

The so-called "fancy chair" did not begin to make its appearance until about 1800. By fancy chair is not meant the finely carved pieces of Chippendale, the Adams, Sheraton or Hepplewhite. The fancy chair was fancy solely because it was painted and decorated with stencilled flowers, leaves, fruit, scenes, etc. Doubtless many of the more prosperous farmers bought such chairs for their wives but, on the whole, the chairs were first made for the middle-class folk.

The vogue of the so-called fancy chair lasted for many years, hanging on until the 1880's in the form of the very comfortable Windsor or Boston rocker. After the 1840's the fancy side or dining room chairs began to wane in the eye of the public, victims of the growing use of the machine that was able to produce more elegant sitting pieces in mahogany and walnut that middle-class people could afford to buy. The fancy chair was gradually abandoned by the middle class and became more widely used in the rural areas.

With the passing of this sort of chair went the fine art of stencilling. True, the work was carried on for many years thereafter, the top rail of Boston rockers being so decorated, but the product was distinctly inferior to the highly perfected and folksy art that was so delightfully executed during the early years of the nineteenth century. The later forms were crude, sloppy, and carelessly applied by production workers who were required to do so many pieces a day or lose their jobs.

Fig. 17. Stencilled top rail of a late Boston rocker of the 1850's. Some of the late rockers of this type had painted floral designs. (Courtesy Florence E. Wright)

This is no place for instruction in stencilling, but a word or two about the subject may not be amiss. The decorations were produced by a series of stencils, each applied in proper sequence. A compote filled with fruit was very popular during the 1830's. In execution, the compote was applied first. Then, piece by piece, came the fruit in the form of pears, peaches, apples, melons, grapes, and leaves until the simple, decorative picture was completed in shades of gold, silver, etc. The backgrounds were usually black, gray, deep brown, or deep green.

Chairs produced by lone workers rather than by the chair factories express more individuality but are also scarcer. It is no exaggeration to say that millions of fancy chairs were produced in the factories during the twenty-five years of the nineteenth century between 1820 and 1845. The year 1820 did not mark the beginning

F IG. 18. (1 and 2) Late debauched types of Windsor chairs made during the 1830's. The one on the left is a writing chair. Later chairs of this type were usually without decorative turning of legs or rungs. (3) Rocking settee or "mammy's bench" as the lady collectors of the day often call it. The fence on the left is re- movable. In place, it was intended to protect the baby. Such set- tees were made with and without rockers. When stationary, they had from six to eight legs. A few were made with as many as ten legs. Such furniture with little change in design was made between 1820's and 1860's. Individual pieces are therefore difficult to date accurately.

of this type of chair but it was the year during which feverish production began.

The fancy chair appeared in a number of different forms. Some were influenced by Sheraton (perhaps most, indeed) some by American Empire and some by the earlier Windsors, as in the case of the Boston rocker.

Along with the fancy side chair there also came the fancy Windsor bench or settee with spindled or slat-back rest and six or eight turned legs. These, too, were stencilled and striped and enjoyed a popularity for twenty-five or more years between 1825 and 1855. They were used in gardens, on porches, and in churches and meeting halls.

There was also the so-called "mammy's bench" or "mammy's rocker" which amounted to a Windsor rocker bench of shorter form. The mother sat at one end while the infant was laid at the other end, a fence (usually detachable) being used to prevent the baby from rolling off. Many of the Windsor settees and cradle rockers as they were called, had solid plank seats with a rolled edge, some had rush seats and some (later perhaps) had cane seats.

Contrary to general belief, the Windsor bench or settee did not belong exclusively to the nineteenth century. It goes back to the latter part of the eighteenth century. So it was in fact with the fancy chair itself but the hand-painted examples coming from the latter part of the eighteenth century are extremely rare and very costly.

Although fancy chairs were made for a number of years before Lambert Hitchcock established his first factory at Barkhamsted, Connecticut, (later called Hitchcockville) about 1818, and although contemporary producers in various parts of the country matched both his quality and production, the man's name has become so firmly attached to this type of chair that he is commonly accepted as its originator. This is unfair to many other men and many other companies who were engaged in the business. However, Hitchcock is now so firmly entrenched in the public mind as the father of the fancy chair that all such chairs whether made by him or not are referred to as "Hitchcock" or "Hitchcock-type" chairs.

FIG. 19. Formal and informal chairs of the 1840's and 1850's. The one on the upper left is a fancy Hitchcock-type with rush seat and so-called "pillow back" top rail. The chair on the lower right is a French importation of the 1850's while the one directly above it is a small Windsor type with plank seat and somewhat "fancy," made for the farm trade during the 1850's.

So far as is known, Hitchcock's first factory produced very few assembled chairs. Rather, he bundled his chair parts and sent them off by ship to Charleston where they were assembled and sold to the southern market for about $1.50 each. Things went so well with Hitchcock that he built a second factory in 1826 where he increased his production and also made finished chairs, including the so-called

Boston rocker and Windsor or fancy settees. It was between 1820 and 1829 that he signed his chairs beneath the seats, "L. Hitchcock, Hitchcockville." Forming a second company in 1832 and taking in his brother-in-law, Arba Alford, he changed the stencil label beneath his chairs to "Hitchcock, Alford & Co., Warranted."

Such a signature today makes what might be an ordinary chair into a rarity worth perhaps as much as $125 when sold as one of a set of four or six. Those who might be interested in such silly (to the writers, at least) indulgence are warned against possible frauds. Hitchcock's marking could be easily duplicated with little fear of detection. After all, every chair stamped with such a signature would be worth an additional hundred dollars. Surely many potential fakers have licked their chops over that prospect!

Not all of the fancy chair forms can be catalogued here. There are variations not only in general design but in turnings, backs, splats, slats, seats, and decorations. Some had plank seats, some had cane seats, and some had rush seats. Some had scrolled top rails, some had plain curved rails, and some had the so-called pillow form. Some back rests were heavily flared and some were not. Some chair backs had spindles, some had stencilled slats, some had stencilled splats.

To the writers' knowledge no one has ever catalogued the various types of fancy chairs in relation to the years that produced them, admittedly a very difficult task in view of the meager data available. Manufacture that ranged from Cincinnati in the Midwest to Vermont, New Hampshire, and Charleston in the East and South, to say nothing of western New York, could not help but produce confusion and subtle complication for the research student. Several thousand different manufacturers and individuals were involved and styles ranged from Sheraton-Federal to Empire, with differences often so slight as to escape the average collector almost entirely.

He should guard against paying a high price for an early type without being sure that it is an early type. He must depend upon the reliability of the dealer with whom he is trading. The chances are that for every ten fancy chairs remaining with us, nine were made subsequent to 1830. Especially wary should the beginning collector be when he is offered a Windsor bench from either the first ten years of the nineteenth century or the last ten years of the eighteenth century. Such articles are extremely rare and practically none exist that have not been heavily restored, a fact sometimes covered up with white, green, or red paint.

FIG. 20. Bamboo type Windsor chair made in the eighteenth century and converted to rocker during the early part of the nineteenth century. Such conversions characterized by wide, scrolled rockers and short projections in rear.

During early Victorian times, Pennsylvania produced a fine brand of fancy chairs intended largely for farm kitchen use. Today we would say that they were "built like battleships." They had plank seats two inches thick and back rests that would have supported anything that P. T. Barnum ever had to offer in the way of fat men.

Information regarding the genesis of the rocking chair is rather foggy. A combination of rumor and research data has it that Ben Franklin was the father of the rocker; that he had a Philadelphia joiner convert one of his chairs by adding rockers to the legs. There is little doubt that Franklin did this but there is a big question as to his having been the first person to order such a contraption. The rocker cradle idea was brought from England by the Pilgrims and it seems strange that over a century and a half passed before any ingenious Yankee thought of adding that comfort to a chair.

FIG. 21. A Mid-Victorian Boston rocker with cane seat but without its original stencilling and striping. On the whole, later Bostons were less well built and proportioned. (Courtesy Florence E. Wright)

Certain it is that Mr. Franklin was not long alone in enjoying this simple luxury after he had the job done in the 1780's. Such conversions were ordered from joiners with increasing frequency during the last of the eighteenth century and, indeed, conversion was popular for many years thereafter, fifty at least.

There is but one quick guide to early rocking chairs and that is not too reliable. The early rockers protruded very little in the rear;

usually about the same in front and rear. An attempt was also made to decorate many such rockers by cutting simple scrolls on their upper edges. Such rockers also tended to be thick and wide; in short, heavy. This holds both for the converted chair and for the true rocking chair, built as such between 1790 and 1820. However, let no novice wager that here and there such heavy rockers were not still made during the 1830's. The field of antiques is no place for the dogmatist. It has had too many already, especially among the new arrivals who never did learn, and perhaps never will, to say, "I'm not sure of the date but I think it might be around ———."

The Boston rocker, which is really a Windsor rocker, first began to appear, in the form in which it is recognized today, around 1825 and in all probability in the city of Boston. Be that as it may, the chair gained quick public favor and, with few changes, none of them major, enjoyed a life that extended from the 1820's to the 1890's.

Needless to say, few of the Bostons produced during the 1820's have come down to the present day although they were able to take a great deal of punishment. A large number are still about that were produced between the 1840's and the 1870's, or later. The earlier ones especially were honestly made chairs even though they were mass-produced. Apparently but few true Boston rockers were individually made. They were mass-produced chairs almost from the time of their introduction, and the joiner working alone could not make them cheaply enough to reach a competitive position.

It is not too difficult to distinguish between the older and later types, although the rules are general and mistakes can easily be made. For one thing, as the years went by there was a progressive deterioration of decoration. The stencil decorations on those produced between 1825 and 1835, and even up to 1840, were usually exquisite examples of this almost lost art. These decorations were of the same high quality and of the same types as used on the ordinary fancy chair. The top rails of the earlier Bostons were also more decorative in shape, being more elaborately scrolled.

As the demand for rocking chairs increased, methods of construc-

FIG. 22. (1) American chair of the Late Empire period (early 1830's). Obviously inspired by French Directoire of the early 1790's. (2) Late Empire fancy chair somewhat in the Sheraton tradition, *Circa* 1835. (3) An early variation of the Windsor rocker, sometimes called the "arrow back" because of the shape of the spindles. Factory-made from the late 1820's to the 1850's. (4) An early type of Windsor or Boston rocker with nicely scrolled top rail. These were invariably stencilled. *Circa* 1830.

tion were simplified. The top rails were made plainer and the stencils, many of them simplified landscapes, became more crude. Still
later (1860's) some of the producers abandoned the slow stencil
work entirely and decorated the chairs with simple striping and a
few random dashes of color on the top slat and on the front of the
seat roll. Some imagination is required to associate such smearing
with anything in either the vegetable or animal kingdom.

FIG. 23.   A comb-back Windsor with the
arrow-shaped spindles. *Circa* about 1820.
(Courtesy Florence E. Wright)

The Boston rocking chair did not wholly dominate the rocker
business even during the last five years of the 1820's. The so-called
arrow-back rocker shown in one of the drawings, although it stood
in the shadow of the Boston, came into more or less general use
especially in New York State and western New England. The stencilling used on such rockers was of admirable variety although it is
rare indeed today to find such a chair with anything but a vestige

of its original decoration. Most of them have been either skinned to their bones and shellacked or covered with a few coats of paint. From a practical viewpoint, they are neither as good looking nor as comfortable as the Boston.

If one frequents antique shops a great deal, he will eventually come upon the knowing lady who is always ready to confide a piece of "inside information" about Boston rockers. "Those with seven spindles are the real early and good ones," she will say. If that were true perhaps most of the Bostons found today would be "the real early and good ones." The fact is that the greatest production of Bostons occurred between 1835 and 1865, and only during the latter part of the Boston rocker era did the six-spindle type appear, the seventh spindle being left out for reasons of economy, no doubt. Ladies who so gladly volunteer such information would be far more useful if they would inform their public about the Bostons with their spindles bent to conform to the back of the sitter. So far as the writers know almost all of the early Bostons boasted of this desirable feature.

So much for fancy chairs and Boston rockers. Next on the agenda comes a general discussion of the more formal types of Victorian and Pre-Victorian chairs. The reader now moves into the stuffy rooms of the upper-middle-class and rich Victorians, those folk who looked down their noses at the (to them) loudly decorated creations offered to their social inferiors, to the people whose hands and backs were helping to make America great.

Unless one is well supplied with cash, the formal chairs made by the better class of cabinetmakers during the early years of the nineteenth century are distinctly in the luxury class. Most of these chairs represent the popular designs that came over into the early years of the nineteenth century from the last few years of the eighteenth century. Both Hepplewhite and Sheraton designs were still popular in the United States, although Mr. Chippendale and the brothers Adam were not doing too well at the time, the Philadelphia Chippendale fever having substantially subsided a number of years before. The Adam boys never were too popular in America even during the height of their fame in England.

The first twenty years of the nineteenth century are rather confusing as a whole, not only in the case of chairs but in furniture in

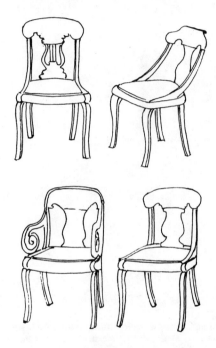

Fig. 24. Four mahogany American chairs of the Late Empire period. Practically all such formal chairs made during the 1830's had slip seats.

general. There was not only some interest in Hepplewhite and Sheraton, but Phyfe with his flair for acceptable originality was also among those present and his designs were being copied by his contemporaries to an extent that makes it difficult to be sure that one is actually looking upon a Phyfe original. Further to confuse this period was the Federal influence, Directoire, and the American version of French Empire (after 1804) with its gradual evolution into a strictly American version. After all, American Empire can be said to have survived in gradually changing form for twenty-five years, or from 1815 to 1840. Some of John Hall's massive designs brought out in the 1840's are often referred to as Late Empire but

FIG. 25. An early Victorian mahogany dining chair with a vase-shaped splat. Chairs of this type are commonly but wrongly called fiddlebacks. (Courtesy Florence E. Wright)

the reference is somewhat shaky. The relationship is based largely on massiveness.

The present discussion of chairs will begin with those available during the 1830's or during the period of Late Empire which was in no sense wholly dominating. The discussion will include chairs, dining room and side chairs; chairs done largely in mahogany or in fine pieces of fiddleback maple, which term refers to the nature of

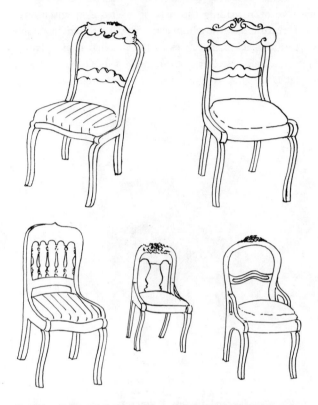

Fig. 26. A few of the many types of Early and Mid-Victorian side chairs. Whereas the legs of many of the Late Empire chairs of the 1830's were inspired by the sweeping curve of the French Directoire, most of the formal side chair legs of the 1840's and later had ogee or cyma curves; a sort of flat-surfaced cabriole. Most of them appeared in mahogany or rosewood and the slip seat of the earlier days was retained.

the grain of the wood and not to the shape of the splat used on some of these chairs. To some, every chair of this period that is equipped with a scrolled splat is a "fiddleback" chair. This is a wholly modern reference and it has been used so loosely as to have lost its meaning, if it ever had one. For many years the present writers have been reading the American and English authorities on antique furniture and never once do they recall having come upon the word fiddleback as it relates to the scrolled back splat of chairs coming from this era. If any readers of this volume come upon a chair splat truly shaped like a fiddle, the writers would appreciate

FIG. 27. An early Victorian mahogany side chair with heavy grape carving and the usual slip seat. A large part of such chairs involved hand labor which accounts for the survival of so many of them. This general type of chair was in wide use. (Courtesy Florence E. Wright)

a photograph of it. Really, the scrolled backs took on all manner of shapes, some of them being pierced.

Many of these chairs (of the 1830's, that is) were influenced by the brief vogue of Regency in England, which was in itself inspired by French Directoire (1793-1804), and some of which may be classed as strictly Late American Empire. Some, too, as the drawings show,

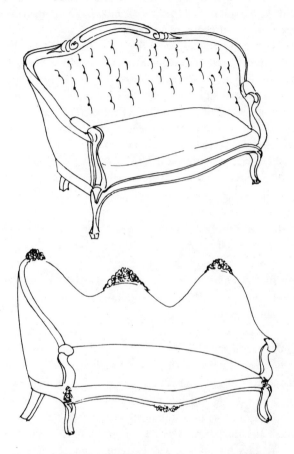

Fig. 28. (Above) A Mid-Victorian love seat with finger
roll carving. The love seat was at one time extremely
popular. Less popular but still to be found are the large
sofas made along similar lines. (Below) A Mid-Victorian
sofa with flower carving on its top rail.

had turned front legs in Sheraton mode and represented what might be called the Greek Revival style of Empire. The detachable or slip seat was used on all chairs of their class.

On the whole, however, it was the designs inspired by the French Directoire more than the designs insisted upon by Napoleon (1804) that influenced chair design in America during the 1820's and 1830's. Most of the formal side chairs produced during the 1830's featured the sweeping curve of the French Directoire chairs in leg design. Duncan Phyfe so often called the master of the curve, borrowed his most-used curve from French Directoire.

The side chairs produced during the 1830's were also good chairs structurally speaking. They were usually produced in the better-class chair factories where the mania for mass manufacture had not become so obvious largely because the mass market for the better class of furniture had not yet developed. Nor is the fact to be overlooked that not a small number of these chairs were carefully and pridefully made by individual joiners.

Many such chairs from this period (1830-1840) were plain, some had simple carving on the top slat or rail, and some had carving on the middle slat, although the Victorian mania for carved fruit and flowers and other nature motifs had not yet arrived. This came during the 1840's and did not expire until the disastrous invasion of the Englishman, Charles Eastlake, in 1870. Especially are the years between 1840 and 1865 noted for such carving in connection with rosewood and mahogany side chairs, as well as love seats and sofas. When the nature motifs were not used, the so-called finger roll was employed, an example of which is shown in one of the drawings in Chapter I. The finger roll was extremely popular from the mid-1840's to the 1860's and was used not only on side chairs but on the so-called lady's and gentleman's chairs, sofas, and love seats.

If there are two articles of furniture that symbolize early and mid-Victorian times more than do the lady's and gentleman's chairs, such articles have not yet been found. But why the "lady's" and "gentleman's" chairs? The lady's chair was armless, not only to

accommodate milady's hoopskirts but also to eliminate any inter-
ference with her handiwork.

Nor is the genesis of such chairs difficult to trace. The type of
wiry cabriole leg used was inspired by the furniture made in France

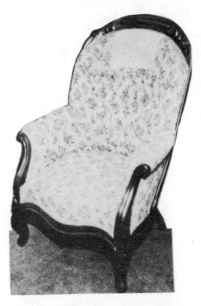

Fig. 29. A Mid-Victorian gentleman's chair with upholstered arms
and wrongly dubbed a Sleepy
Hollow by modern collectors of
Victorian things. These appeared
with finger roll, flower, fruit, and
nut carvings on the top rail.

during the reign of Louis XV. While it is generally assumed that
these styles were not revived in this country until early Victorian
times, recent research would appear to cast some doubt on this
stand. Careful investigation by the president of a large Grand
Rapids furniture company leaves one with the impression that the
first of the chairs in question and the first of the Louis XV revival

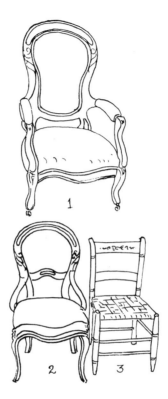

Fɪɢ. 30. (1) A gentleman's chair with so-called corset back. The backs of both lady's and gentleman's chairs were either oval or one of the types illustrated. They were popular between the years 1845 and 1870, although later types with shallow machine carvings on their rails can be found. The earlier and better chairs of this sort were made in mahogany, rosewood, and walnut and all were hand-carved either with the finger rolls or with flowers, fruit, or nuts on the top rails. (2) A finger roll side chair of the 1850's, and (3) its contemporary country cousin, one of the many hundreds of thousands of the cruder types of fancy chairs that appeared during the 1850's.

took place in a small cabinetmaker's shop in Virginia sometime during the early 1820's. Apparently this first attempt at revival had only local success, for it was more than twenty years before the first of the early Victorian lady's and gentleman's chairs began to appear in the better-class homes.

Although the prices asked for such chairs have long since reached ridiculous levels, one must remember that this results from demand

FIG. 31. A Mid-Victorian version of the Louis XV bergère tabouret where a chair and a seat-high stool or tabouret form a chaise longue. Seat-high stools of this type are difficult to find, although smaller ones in the Victorian Louis XV style are not.

rather than from scarcity. These prices are still substantially lower than those asked for the finer pieces produced during the first twenty years of the nineteenth century. So plentiful indeed is such Victorian furniture that it is not too difficult for a collector to assemble a complete and matching living room suite, especially in the case of the finger roll motif.

One of the rarest and most difficult to find of the Louis XV revival articles is the tabouret used with the lady's chair to form a chaise longue. There are footstools of this type, to be sure, but these must not be confused with the true tabouret which matches the lady's chair in height and width and in legs, as will be seen in the photographs.

Lady's and gentleman's chairs were made in steadily diminishing numbers until perhaps as late as 1875, but the later ones were of inferior quality both in construction and design. Instead of being

FIG. 32. Early and Mid-Victorian footstools with scrolled, turned, and cabriole legs. Formal stools were invariably of mahogany, rosewood, or walnut and supplied with upholstered tops. Their country counterparts, made principally for keeping one's feet off cold, draughty floors while sitting, were made of hickory, oak, cherry, or maple with peg legs, and were often called "crickets."

carved with roses, fruit, or finger rolls, the later ones were carved with shallow lines cut by newly invented machinery.

Occasionally one comes upon a chair of the lady's type equipped with rockers. So far as the writers know, no lady's chairs were originally made with rockers. In most such cases it will also be found that the rockers were added within the memory of surviving members of a family.

The so-called Lincoln rocker is a rocker in its own right, the first of them appearing probably in the late 1840's or early 1850's. At any rate President Lincoln admired these chairs, a fact discovered

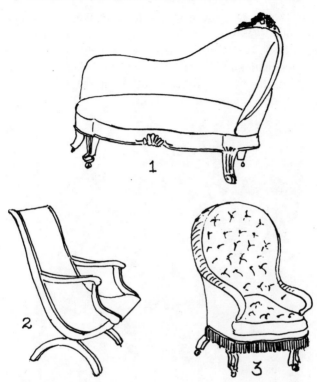

Fig. 33. (1) A Grecian sofa of the mid-1840's, a piece of furniture popular before the so-called love seat but used throughout the Victorian period in one form or another. (2) A true Sleepy Hollow chair of the late 1840's. The gentleman's chairs with upholstered arms are today wrongly called Sleepy Hollows. (3) A typical Mid-Victorian upholstered chair usually characterized with heavy fringe. Such chairs being more perishable than other chairs because of complete fabric covering are today very scarce except in very late designs.

by the manager of the Ford Theater in Washington, D.C., who thereupon moved one of these chairs from the lounge of the theater office to the presidential box. Lincoln was sitting in this chair when shot by the assassin, Booth.

Any reference to American furniture produced between the years

1845 and 1856 cannot, out of justice if not admiration, overlook the work of John Henry Belter. Apparently the Metropolitan Museum of Art in New York City has taken Belter under its wing as being most representative of the Mid-Victorian period. At least the two Victorian rooms at the Museum shown in the photographs are heavy with Belter, especially his chairs.

FIG. 34. A fine example of John Belter in his best dress; a Belter sofa of the 1850's with pierced-carved top rail. (Courtesy Metropolitan Museum of Art, New York City)

It was Belter who invented plywood in 1856, gluing several thicknesses of rosewood together, with the grain at variance, the result being strong and most useful for his type of pierced carving. The idea was patented and Belter employed it for many years in his factory at 76th Street and Third Avenue, New York City. This factory was an outgrowth of his great popularity among people of wealth who "had all of their taste in their mouth," as the saying goes.

Belter was a master craftsman in everything but design. He was able to carve wood as easily as other men might carve a piece of wax or soap. His joinery, too, was beyond reproach; he had learned his trade in the state of Württemberg, Germany. Although the stuffed shirt section of the antique trade may shudder at the mere thought, Belter's early joinery was every bit as good in its own way as that of Saint Goddard or Saint Townsend of Rhode Island, or Saint Savery of Philadelphia. During his factory years Belter employed as many as one hundred men, not a few of them German immigrants, all skillful with carving chisels.

One cannot begin to list the side chair variations and minor styles current between the years 1840 and 1870, the period of chief interest to any collector of Victorian. A book easily the size of this would be needed for a mere catalogue. Further to complicate the scene, there is the French furniture imported into Boston, New York, and Philadelphia during the reign of Napoleon III. Some English furniture was also imported during these years.

Perhaps the best the reader can do is carefully to examine the accompanying drawings and the photographs to fix in his mind the general types of side chairs popular between the years 1830 and 1870 and to be guided accordingly. One should not try to rivet down any piece of furniture to any particular year, and this is especially true of chairs.

Many collectors of Victorian feel that the Early and Mid-Victorian periods must have been without completely upholstered chairs. This is not true but it is rare indeed to find a truly authentic sample of such chairs in the antique shops and the reason is not hard to find. These chairs were more perishable than other types. It may also be assumed that good housewives would object to their being stored in attics after they were worn and replaced by new ones; they offered excellent nesting places for mice and moths. In all probability, a great number of them were therefore destroyed in trash fires, accounting for their present scarcity. Certainly it is known that they were widely used, hardly a Victorian parlor being without one or two.

Fig. 35. Top and middle: Mid-Victorian sofas. The bottom sofa was an Early Victorian affair produced about 1845 at the very latest and obviously indebted to the furniture designs created by the Baltimore architect, John Hall.

These chairs were more comfortable by far than anything else the early and mid-Victorians had to sit upon. Not a few of them were also in fairly good taste, with expensive coverings in damask and heavily fringed skirts. Even the bare frames and springs are difficult to find these days.

The kitchen and dining room chairs made for the provincial trade after 1860 were pretty bad, barring the Boston rocker which, although not as good as the chairs of former years, was still acceptable. Gone, too, were the charming fancy chairs of the earlier days and in came the ugly things chewed into dubious being by the wood-hungry machinery of the new factories. These chairs are still about, thousands of them. Some day, if they last long enough, the mantle of respectable antiquity will settle down upon them as it will on the Eastlake monstrosities that came subsequent to 1870. How fortunate it is that only the very young among us will be called upon for acknowledgments!

CHAPTER IV

Victorian Chests and Secretaries

THE chests and secretaries made by the Early and Mid-Victorian cabinetmakers and furniture factories are among the most acceptable things produced by the whole Victorian era. That statement is by no means made as a blanket endorsement; not all of these chests and secretaries were good, but the percentage of good ones was fair. However, as in the case of all Victorian furniture, the workmanship of the factory-made pieces was usually poor, and even when good was only moderately good, especially when compared with the workmanship of the cabinetmakers of the period before. Indeed the whole of the nineteenth century suffered progressive deterioration in all of the crafts. Men were in a hurry and craftsmen lost their pride in their work.

As in other cases, a slight violation of the title of our book will be indulged in by a return to the year when Queen Victoria took her throne. Practically all of the chests produced before 1820 were still marked by eighteenth century inspiration. For all practical purposes Chippendale and the brothers Adam had expired before the turn of the century, but this was not the case with Sheraton and Hepplewhite. If Chippendale persisted at all he was to be found in the scrolled bracket feet of country chests in pine or other soft woods. Indeed, in that manner he continued for many a year; of the Early and Mid-Victorian chests in formal dress many boasted such feet.

The Hepplewhite type of bureau or chest was usually finely proportioned (narrow compared with its length) and made in walnut, cherry, maple, or mahogany, often with fine pencil-line inlay around the drawer fronts. Sometimes the feet were splayed

Fig. 36. Early American Empire (1810) with over-hanging top drawer and classical columns. This type of chest is scarce and difficult to find.

(flared outward) and sometimes the simple form of Hepplewhite bracket was used. Drawer pulls were of the bail type with oval pressed brass plates having beehives, thistles, eagles, acorns, sheaves of wheat, or baskets of fruit as a center decoration.

The earlier Sheraton bureaus, between 1800 and 1810-15, that is, usually had bow fronts and no galleries. Such chests can never be mistaken for anything else because of the reeded corner columns that went straight to the top of the chest. Eventually, however, the Empire fashion brought changes to the Sheraton bureau. Many if not most of those made between 1815 and 1825 boasted a scrolled backboard, and the corner columns had spiraled reeding, instead of vertical.

While almost all Hepplewhite and Sheraton bureaus of this period were made in the finer cabinet woods, there are also many lovely examples to be found in figured maple, choice articles indeed.

If the reader will for a moment consider the general design of the true French Empire bureau, that is the design which was approved by the Emperor himself, he will be able thereafter easily to recognize any American bureau as such and to determine whether it was Late or Early Empire.

Outstanding among the easily recognized characteristics of the Empire type bureau or chest is the overhanging top drawer. This appeared on the first of the Empire chests made in France and it persisted until the last of the Late Empire chests were made here in America during the later 1830's.

On either side of the Napoleon Empire pieces made in France, there appeared a classical column rather heavy and usually in tapered square form. These gave the appearance of supporting the overhanging top drawer, and the top of each column was adorned with the head of a sphinx as part of the inspiration that Napoleon brought to France after his successful Egyptian campaign. Moderately heavy claw feet appeared in the front of the chest only. Some French chests also adapted the Doric type or tapered round column with capitals or tops of carved leaves. This was usually the type of column found on the earliest chests of American Empire. Such columns were used with gradually diminishing popularity until 1825 but the design was not totally abandoned. Rather it was cheapened in the interests of greater production, the curse of the whole period which followed.

As an example of the laxity in workmanship and the tendency to take short cuts in making furniture, the writers mention the growing tendency of cabinetmakers to make use of the pilaster. The pilaster is a semiround column glued or nailed to either side of the front of a chest, clock, etc. Early Empire chests, for example, had turned columns, and a whole column was used on each side. Then later some cabinetmakers turned a single column and sawed it in two lengthwise, using a half on either side of the chest. This made it

Fig. 37. A Late American Empire chest characterized by heavily carved mahogany columns and claw feet. Such chests are not scarce but they bring good prices. Drawer fronts were usually crotch mahogany veneer. *Circa* 1825.

necessary for the cabinetmaker to turn only one column on his lathe. Naturally, all things considered, the best type of Early American Empire has two whole Doric or other columns mounted beneath the overhanging top drawer, with a small space between them and the front of the chest. The pilaster idea probably started sometime during the 1820's and persisted until the early 1840's, dying slowly after having served as a hackneyed decorative device for many years.

Early chests of American Empire with the smooth-surface Doric columns are scarce and expensive. It was not long after their advent that the more truly American version of French Empire began to appear, probably in the early 1820's or before. The Doric column, as set forth from the chest, began to be replaced by the heavily

FIG. 38. A bureau desk wrongly called a butler's secretary. This type of desk in Sheraton and Empire was very popular between the years 1820-35. (Courtesy Mrs. George Carnochan, Lewiston, N. Y.)

carved column with acanthus leaf motif. (It must be remembered, however, that the Doric column persisted for many years thereafter, in pilaster form.) As in the case of the early Doric columns, two whole carved columns were used on each chest together with heavy claw feet, the columns being mounted with a small space between them and the chest front.

It was not long before the cabinetmakers, who probably spent days carving out the columns, decided that one completely carved column was enough, whereupon they sawed the completed column in half lengthwise and mounted the halves as pilasters. Such chests also appear with the pineapple motif worked in.

One cannot say that after such-and-such a date, on all American Empire chests with carved pillars, the pillars were pilaster type. There were cabinetmakers who would not stoop to such slipshod methods. Needless to say, the chests with the whole columns are by far the most desirable and the purest in form. However, let no collector waste too much of his or her time searching for such chests with anything but mahogany or mahogany veneer as wood. Such things are very scare, although an occasional one in cherry may be found. Naturally one cannot blame the cabinetmakers for shying away from hard, figured maple as a medium for carving!

This might be a good place to set down a word or two about the misnamed "butler's secretary." This is a misnomer for a desk in the form of a bureau which was popular during the first third of the nineteenth century. When closed, such a desk appeared as an ordinary bureau or chest; perhaps in Hepplewhite, perhaps in Empire with carved columns, plain columns, or pilaster columns, or in spiral reeding with what might be called a Sheraton-Empire flavor. A simulated top drawer front, which was large compared with the actual drawer fronts below, dropped forward to form a writing surface and to reveal a tier of pigeonholes. This was a bureau desk intended for ordinary use as a desk and not as a butler's secretary, as such desks are now commonly called.

The butler's secretary was an integral part of the more massive and expensive American Empire sideboards with their heavy pillars, etc. The center top drawer of these sideboards was only simulated. When it was pulled down it, too, formed a writing surface and revealed pigeonholes wherein the butler might place his bills and file his menus after they had been approved by the mistress of the house. The bureau desk reached well into the 1830's as did the sideboard with butler's secretary.

The question may now be fairly asked, "What were the country folk doing about their chests during the early part of the nineteenth century?" As has been stated before, the shift from period to period does not occur overnight. In so far as provincial furniture is concerned, changes were beginning to appear as early as 1790. The Windsor chairs were farther and farther away from the lovely types produced in Philadelphia during the 1760's, and chests of

FIG. 39. One of the better types of Late Empire sideboards, many of which, when made by the better class of cabinetmakers, owed no apologies to the best workmanship of the eighteenth century. This is true of all of the earlier and better class cabinetmaking of the early part of the nineteenth century. The center section with the two large ring pulls drops forward, forming a desk and uncovering pigeonholes. This is a true butler's secretary.

drawers began to lose some of the quaint Chippendale effects of earlier times. There was no change in wood; pine, tulipwood, maple, and cherry were still the favorites, with an occasional walnut piece. However, there was a noticeable trend toward simplicity of design and short cuts in making things.

The typical pine, maple, or cherry chest between 1800 and the

1830's was rather high (about forty-two inches) compared with the later Victorian pieces and it was rather narrow, say about eighteen to twenty inches, and long (forty-two inches). Whereas many of the earlier provincial chests (both high and low) of the eighteenth century had dovetailed corners and were therefore strong and sturdy, precious few of the nineteenth century fellows had either the time or the inclination to fuss with such precise joinery. That is not to say that these joints were ruled out completely. They are simply scarce as nineteenth century types.

The typical pine chest of the first twenty-five years of the nineteenth century had usually from three to four drawers, the top drawer doubtless intended for blankets and therefore deeper than the others. Oftentimes the drawers were graduated in size, the lowest one being smallest. Oftentimes, too, the drawer edges were delicately lipped with a molding plane, and the drawer fronts were very thick, more than one inch.

End and top boards were invariably single wide boards. If one is asked to purchase a pine, maple, or cherry chest as being from a period prior to 1840 and that chest has top or end boards formed of several components glued together, then one has every right to be very suspicious. The old fellows shied away from such shoddy construction.

Invariably the end boards of these early provincial chests went straight down to the floor, their lower corners being scrolled in some manner to serve as part of a bracket foot. Handmade molding was usually placed around the skirt at a point just below the bottom drawer.

There is ample reason to believe that the width of all provincial chests made in America during early times and up to the 1840's or later was determined by the width of the pine, cherry, or maple boards available to the cabinetmakers. They insisted that both the tops of such chests and the end boards be made of single boards.

Early pine, maple, walnut, mahogany, and cherry blanket chests— that is those coming down from the eighteenth century—were low and provided with a lid. Some had small drawers underneath the

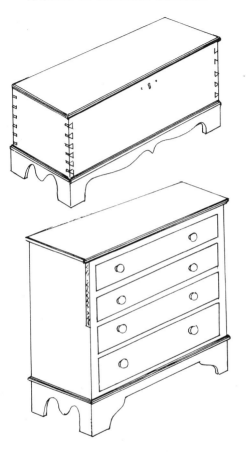

Fig. 40. (Top) Simple pine blanket chest
of the early nineteenth century with dovetailed corners. Such chests in pine, cherry,
maple, and walnut were made in rural
America well into Victorian times. They
are difficult to date. (Bottom) An early
nineteenth century tall blanket chest in pine
with lid top, the first two drawer fronts
being simulated. Made up to and beyond
early Victorian times.

blanket well; practically all had bracket feet, some nicely scrolled and molded in the Chippendale manner, some not. In forms that were gradually less desirable, such blanket chests were made into

Fig. 41. A typical John Hall chest practically copied from his book of designs. Overhanging, ogee top drawer, pressed-glass pulls, scrolled feet, and crotch mahogany veneer. *Circa* 1845.
(Courtesy Florence E. Wright)

the 1870's. However, during the latter part of the eighteenth century, the tall blanket chest began to appear. This took the form of a regular chest of drawers save that the top formed a lid and the blanket compartment beneath it took up the space of two ordinary

F IG. 42. (Top) John Hall chest of the 1840's as compared with (lower) a cheap chest of the 1880's. The latter had T-drop pulls and raised drawer front covered with crotch walnut veneer. It was usually made of walnut, while the Early Victorian chests were usually of other woods with crotch mahogany veneer.

drawers. In the better chests of this type, the cabinetmaker simulated drawer fronts on the top front of the chest, the lower two drawers being real. Lid tops were edged with hand-cut molding that overlapped the top of the chest body when the lid was down, thereby sealing the crevice against moths. Such chests were made by the thousands and stoutly enough to permit many of them to survive until this day. They are excellent property. Especially desirable are those with dovetail joints. The same holds for the low blanket chest.

Returning to the subject of the more formal types of chests in the more acceptable cabinet woods, we reach the era of John Hall (1840-1850). His chests were no different from other pieces de-

Fig. 43. A chest relic of Civil War days. Chamfered corners with vase-turned pilasters, scrolled feet, and two small drawers on top.

signed by him and made by the early furniture manufacturers, from Boston to Charleston. They had drawer fronts veneered in mahogany, heavy scrolled feet, heavy scrolled brackets to replace the Empire pillar, a shallow overhanging top drawer usually with an ogee front, thick slab tops, and panelled ends. The back legs were heavy and of turned wood. Not infrequently sycamore was used for these chest tops. Some such chests had mirror frames, most did not. Some, too, were equipped with choice Sandwich knobs, some were not. Most had knobs of turned mahogany. Indeed, the whole of the Early and Mid-Victorian periods were marked by the extensive use of the turned wooden knob in either walnut or mahogany and these even on some of the best furniture of the day. The turned wooden knob indeed has a record that dates from early times down to this very day. There was a time during the 1870's when the carved leaf drawer pull was very popular, but it never completely destroyed the market for the plain turned knob.

FIG. 44. A Late Empire chest of the so-called "chimney top" type, with overhanging top drawers, pilaster pillars, curly maple veneer, and sandwich knobs. *Circa* 1835-40.

Let it not be assumed that all of the chests turned out by the furniture houses during the 1840's paid homage to the highly debatable genius of John Hall as a furniture designer. Many were the more discriminating souls who must have turned from him in disgust to have a local cabinetmaker supply their needs. Nor did all of the furniture houses follow Hall exclusively. Unfortunately the writers cannot catalogue all of the variations of the 1840-1850 period

Fig. 45. Pure Eastlake in the more grotesque form as produced in 1875. This was the culmination of all the mistakes made by the Victorian furniture designers. Badly proportioned, gawky, knobby, and with crotch walnut veneer. It was made for the carriage trade and was very expensive. (Courtesy Grand Rapids Furniture Museum)

here. On the whole, however, the non-Hall types of chests were superior from a design viewpoint although no manufacturers took too much pains about superior construction.

Quick to gain favor about this time and to persist with but slight variations until the disastrous dawn of Eastlake, was the plain type of chest shown among the illustrations as coming from this period.

It usually had two small drawers set back on the top, intended perhaps for handkerchiefs and other small accessories. In later forms the two drawers were below the top rather than on it and they were flush with the rest of the drawers. Really, the two small drawers mounted on top of the chest and having less length by one-half than the regular-sized drawers beneath the top, was not a new idea. Many of the Late Empire chests had such accessory drawers, usually chests of a sort of halfhearted Sheraton type. The Victorian counterpart, however, had no carving of any sort unless one can call the machine-cut piecrust molding used on many such chests carving. This molding was usually attached near the bottom and sometimes along both top and bottom on both sides and front.

Some of these chests were in walnut veneer, some in mahogany veneer. All of the veneering was good, many of the veneer patterns being exquisite. Usually the drawer fronts were of soft pine because this held the veneer best. Keyhole escutcheons were usually of brass, less frequently of diamond-shaped ivory.

Sometimes the skirt (nethermost board across the front of the chest between the feet) was nicely scrolled, sometimes straight. Invariably the scrolled bracket foot was employed, most of them owing very little to Mr. Chippendale but still not too bad.

As time went on, these chests, by far the best that the Victorian period had to offer as its very own, underwent rather severe change. During the 1860's they began to appear with chamfered corners (the ladies might call them bevelled corners) to which knobby pilasters were glued. Needless to say these added nothing to the beauty of such chests.

The 1860's also brought another innovation in a furniture world that was so soon to become "innovated" into a nightmare. In place of the two small top drawers set back from the front edge of the chest, the drawers were separated, one placed on each side of the chest top and the drawers having the same length as the other drawers which brought them out flush with them. This was not a contribution in the interests of beauty or good design.

If the reader wishes a secretary that will avoid most of the artless devices used by Victorian designers and makers, his purchase will have to be limited to the years between the latter 1830's and 1870. Of course he may go back to the early part of the century but his purchase will not be Victorian. The writers are now thinking only of a well-appointed Victorian room. Some collectors relish admixtures of periods, some do not. There is a certain satisfaction in building up a room of a definite period whatever that period may be.

FIG. 46. Two "lesser evil" chests.appearing in the photograph in the salesman's catalogue of Breed and Company, Jamestown, New York, about 1872. They were quoted to the trade at $16 and $18 each.

In so far as Victorian is concerned, the years between 1840 and 1855 are no doubt the best from which to choose, since they include things that were perhaps in better taste and are without overdone stuffiness and trashy bric-a-brac. Certainly 1870 is a deadline, if a deadline has to be fixed and if one is to avoid the mass murder of taste that was introduced with Eastlake's Medieval Gothic. Gothic appeared before Eastlake's book but it was Eastlake who gave the movement its great impetus.

John Hall's secretaries of the 1840's were not too bad—some of

Fig. 47. A provincial type secretary of the handmade class. These were all of the same general type, differing only in details and all marked by stark simplicity. During the 1840's, when the one shown above was made, such secretaries appeared more often in walnut, maple, and cherry than in pine.

them, that is. The better ones were low and rather squatty, to be sure, and they were also extremely heavy. Yet they "had something about them" that is not easily defined. Perhaps one might call it substantial dignity. Certainly they were not fussy or overloaded with decorative devices as were many of the later secretaries. On the whole, they were severely plain and with a form of construction as good as any of the early Victorian pieces. More often than not,

FIG. 48. One of the more desirable of the Early Victorian secretaries in mahogany and mahogany veneer. It may be said of the 1840's in general that the secretaries made during these years were the most acceptable of all those made in Victorian times.

they were without glass fronts or doors, the front being of veneered mahogany and dropping to form the writing shelf. Some had a single bookshelf behind the drop, two or three small drawers, and a few pigeonholes. Top drawers of the lower or chest section usually had an ogee, mahogany veneered front, while the drawers below this were larger and also had fronts covered with veneering.

Fɪɢ. 49. A typical John Hall, drop front secretary of the 1840's shown with out-of-period brasses. Such secretaries were characterized by heavy, scrolled feet, crotch mahogany veneer, and total lack of carving in any form.
Circa 1845.

It was during the latter 1840's that other types of plain combination secretaries and bookcases began to arrive. They owed little or nothing to Hall's doubtful genius, but were sedate and in fairly good taste. Certainly they boasted none of the ugly ornamentation that came later. They usually had two glass doors with or without dividers, and the top cornice was plain mahogany veneer placed over pleasantly carved surfaces and perfectly plain ones. Some had

FIG. 50. A late walnut secretary-book-case made in the early ·1870's and equipped with carved leaf drawer pulls. All late Victorian secretaries were taller by a foot or more than were the earlier ones. (Courtesy Florence E. Wright)

drawers in the chest bottom and others (in the minority) had doors of solid wood.

More frequently, however, one comes upon secretaries made after 1870 with the two bottom doors covering shelves. By this time, all secretaries were higher and less well proportioned largely because of the vogue for high ceiling rooms that set in during the late

1850's when more plentiful heating arrived. Come the 1870's, heating plants could be located centrally in the basement to replace the ornamental parlor stoves sitting on their zinc pads, which were there to catch the ash during shaking or cleaning. The parlor stove

FIG. 51. Dresser chest and commode of the early 1870's, both with white marble tops and carved leaf drawer pulls. Beginning with the late 1860's, most chests were provided with long mirrors with emphasis on use of walnut for the better-class furniture and chestnut for the cheaper stuff. This photo is copied from what was perhaps the first photographic salesman's catalogue used in the furniture trade. It was produced by Breed and Company, of Jamestown, New York, about 1872.

started the vogue for high ceilings and the central heating plant perpetuated it.

The collector should not overlook the quaint little secretaries that were custom made between the years 1840 and 1865. Small town cabinetmakers, many of them of the old school, were still alive and at work producing a considerable number of choice pieces. The present writers have seen many secretaries that have come from their shops. Although in general conformity with the styles of the day, these secretaries have individual touches that place most of them quite apart. For one thing, most by far were not veneered. Indeed mahogany was rarely used, in any form. The woods employed were cherry, maple, and walnut, pine being quite a rarity save in truly provincial pieces. Considerable searching will be required for finding a pine piece of this sort.

After 1870, but by no means exclusively assigned to this period, the marble-topped chest became immensely popular, with walnut as the wood. Walnut was also popular in the mid-1840's but it reached the peak of public acceptance during the 1870's. It was also during the latter part of the 1870's that chestnut was introduced for use in the cheaper bedroom suites. This was usually finished in a light "golden" color. The chestnut chests were rather plain, mostly without marble tops, and usually with machine-carved drawer pulls in leaf form.

Those without experience in refinishing antique furniture are advised to shy away from chestnut chests. Chestnut has a prominent and deep grain not particularly beautiful and very difficult to fill. Only disappointment will result from any attempt, either amateur or professional, to refinish such surfaces.

It was during the mid-1870's that a form of rather pleasant bedroom furniture came to market. How this furniture managed entirely to escape the Eastlake scourge is not known. It was called Cottage Furniture and was very plain, painted in light colors such as buff and pearl, and decorated with transfers of scenes or flowers. In some cases, the scenes or flowers were hand painted.

If one can find a whole bedroom suite of this kind of furniture with the picture decorations in a good state of preservation it is indeed worth buying. It must be confessed, however, that such furniture is not in good supply and never has been. For one thing there has been no great demand for it, although it is the only furniture from the 1870's and 1880's that was done in any sort of acceptable taste. The chests, both small and large, and the commodes were usually made of pine.

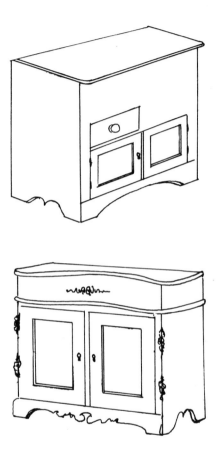

Fig. 52. (Top) Walnut commode of the late 1870's with lift top revealing well in which washbowl and waterpitcher were stored. Bottom intended for chambermug and slopjar. (Below) A more acceptable marble top commode of the early 1860's.

The Victorians were very "commode conscious," one might say. They had to be, what with the necessity of providing concealment for the unspeakable chambermug as well as a place to serve as a washstand and to hold the huge china waterpitcher, washbowl, soapdish, etc.

The usual form of the commode was that of a small chest, with two swinging doors covering the compartment for the storage of the slopjar and chambermug, a small top drawer, and spindles mounted horizontally at either end of the top to serve as towelracks. Perhaps it was the advisability of using marble tops for such commodes and washstands that was responsible for introducing marble top bedroom furniture on a large scale during the late 1860's and the 1870's.

Another type of commode used in the 1870's and early 1880's had a lift top of wood. The wood was usually walnut or chestnut. These commodes were of the cheaper class of furniture, the more expensive ones of this period being supplied with marble tops. When the lid of such a commode was opened it uncovered a deep well occupying the whole top section of the piece. This was intended for the storage of the toilet set when not in use, being deep enough to accommodate the large waterpitchers along with washbowls. Such commodes had only a single small drawer and the lower section had two swinging doors used to cover the chambermug on one side and the slopjar on the other. Because the well in the top of such commodes is deep enough to accommodate liquor bottles, they are often purchased nowadays to serve as liquor cabinets.

The marble top era of American bedroom furniture was indeed a dreary one. Why the sleepers of those days were not more troubled with nightmares than they were is not known. Certainly there was enough inspiration about. The dressers became huge, and were heavily and fearfully carved and supplied with tall looking glasses topped with monstrous cornices. They were invariably in walnut, with crotch-walnut veneering on the drawer fronts. Drawer pulls on the more expensive types were of the tear drop or t-type drop varieties, both being heavy and ugly.

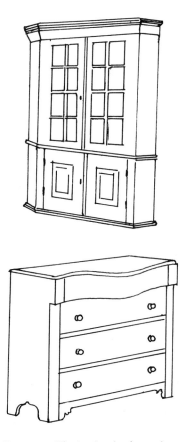

FIG. 53. (Top) A simple walnut
corner cupboard of the general type
known to have been made in rural
districts during Early Victorian times.
Most, however, were in cherry, some
in maple. (Lower) A simple chest of
the late 1850's with overhanging bow
front top drawer and crotch mahogany veneer on all drawer fronts.

For those who wish to escape all of the factory-made bedroom furniture of the 1840's, 1850's, and 1860's, there can be a measure of relief. Not too infrequently one finds custom-made chests coming down from these years. They are put together better and they carry those little touches of individuality that mark them off from the general run of things. Some are in maple, some in walnut or cherry, and (more rarely) in pine. If one finds such a chest in pine it is

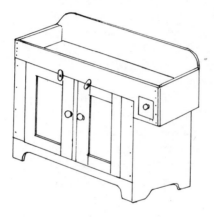

FIG. 54. A so-called dry sink in pine. These were used over a relatively wide period and are very difficult to date. By far the larger number of those still in existence were made during the last half of the nineteenth century.

usually primitive in style, starkly utilitarian, and fit only for a primitive bedroom. Many have been the primitive pine, cherry, and maple chests of the years mentioned above that have been sold to gullible ladies as eighteenth century pieces, and this at prices usually paid for the older things.

One must have pity upon the collector of Victorian furniture in his or her search for acceptable corner cupboards of this period. Apparently the corner cupboard was not a favorite article of furniture among the Victorians. For every Victorian corner cupboard there are still to be found five such cupboards from the eighteenth century. It seems that these cupboards gradually lost their standing in the urban centers by the 1840's although they were still popular in the provinces. Here and there one finds an Early Victorian or a Late Empire corner cupboard, the latter done in mahogany and mahogany veneer, but they are scarce.

Still another provincial piece that might be mentioned here is the pine, walnut, maple, or cherry dresser or Welsh cupboard affair often found in Early and Mid-Victorian farmstead dining rooms and kitchens. One will never know how many hundreds of these articles have been palmed off on unsuspecting ladies as eighteenth century rarities. They are still to be had if one will but take the time to search them out.

Although the so-called dry sink is box furniture and not strictly speaking a chest, comment might be made here concerning it. It is usually a pine article and very provincial in nature. Such sinks, it should be pointed out, were made and used on farms well up into the 1890's and most of those that have been sold miss the right to be called antiques by as many as forty or fifty years.

CHAPTER V

Tables

THERE was a table or stand in every Victorian room: dining room, kitchen, parlor, and bedroom. They ranged in size from the massive boards of the big-family farms to the often delicate and well-proportioned bedside affairs with their one or two drawers as often as not fitted with fine examples of early pressed-glass knobs. Some of these had turned legs, some (especially the earlier ones) had tapered square legs, and some were both squared and turned, being square in the mid-section and turned at the lower ends and at the upper ends below the point where the table side and end boards were mortised into them.

Especially desirable from almost every point of view, design, workmanship, etc., are the simple tables produced during the first quarter of the nineteenth century, a large number of which were made for tavern use. The years between 1800 and 1845 were indeed the years of the tavern. Not that they were new, but numerous. The population of the country was growing rapidly and travel was largely by foot, stage, or horseback. As the great network of canals and railroads began to spread out over the Eastern and Midwestern sections of the country, taverns became less necessary. The packet-boat traveller slept on board and the rail traveller had no need to leave his coach until he arrived at his destination.

The well-established tavern had several varieties of tables, all of them in the hard or semihard woods like cherry and maple. By far the most numerous were the small tavern tables made to serve one or two. These could be pushed about easily; shoved close to the fireplace, for instance, when some chilled and snow-covered traveller sought bait (as it was said in those days) for his horse, shelter and comfort for himself.

Many of the early nineteenth century taverns, of course, were equipped with eighteenth century furniture and it was so for many years until they gradually went out of business. Those who began

FIG. 55. A sewing or work stand made during the 1840's and equipped with rare type of pressed brass pulls. Covered with crotch mahogany, save top and leaves. (Authors' collection)

keeping tavern in the early part of the nineteenth century usually started anew with tables that had more of a nineteenth century flavor about them. Gone were the fine gate-legs with turned legs and turned stretchers. In their places came the rather plain cherry, maple, and walnut tables, often not identifiable as to influence on design but some having a whiff of Hepplewhite in the tapered legs.

The primitive tables of this era (say 1810 to 1840) were difficult to classify, those in the East being different from those in the West, etc. America was growing up, spreading out, and so were ideas.

Some of the very choice Pembroke mahogany tables as well as Hepplewhite and Sheraton type card or game tables were made during the first twenty or twenty-five years of the nineteenth century. The same held for dining room tables and especially for the

Fig. 56. Work- or sewing table of Early Victorian period but copied after a colonial design save the turtle feet. (Collection of Mrs. George Carnochan, Lewiston, N. Y.)

two- and three-piece banquet tables made for those swells of the day who entertained lavishly.

Especially delightful were the little work tables and bedside tables of those days. Many of the earliest nineteenth century examples were either pretty pure Sheraton or else Hepplewhite and today demand heavy prices, so heavy indeed as to be beyond the purse of the average collector of Victorian.

Gradually these finer types of tables began to be replaced by Early Empire, which was massive enough but the first types of which were minus the heavy carving that later came to mark furniture bearing this label. The heavy mahogany pillar so characteristic of all Empire including Napoleon's personal furniture, was indeed present but the body of the pillar or column had a plain uncarved

FIG. 57. (1) Provincial type bedside stand made between 1820's and 1850's. (2) A John Hall type stand or worktable with veneered drawer front, pedestal, and feet. *Circa* 1845. (3) Sheraton type stand. Could have been made between the 1820's and 1840's. (4) Provincial type cherry or maple stand from the 1830's, 1840's, or even later.

surface. It was during the 1820's that the deeply and heavily carved American Empire stuff came forth; and the penchant for carving lasted well into the 1830's. Thus Late American Empire, as the term relates to mahogany dressers, tables, and the like, is represented by deep carving, much of it with the acanthus leaf as chief motif.

If one wishes a Late Empire dining room in mahogany there can be but two principal choices for an appropriate table. Still fairly plentiful and not too expensive are the beautiful mahogany drop-leaf tables. These are more common with four than with six legs, not too large in diameter, and on the whole nicely carved and provided with brass cup casters. One should never live to regret an investment in such a piece of furniture. These tables were well made

Fig. 58. Drop-leaf mahogany table of Empire design and with carved mahogany pedestal. Probably made sometime between 1820 and 1830. (Courtesy Florence E. Wright)

of well-selected, well-seasoned stock and if one likes American Empire in its later form, here indeed is something that is bound to please. Some of the table legs are carved with the acanthus leaf motif, some with spiral reeding.

Such tables were apparently available to middle-class families in the latter part of the 1820's and persisted with diminishing popularity throughout most of the 1830's.

Choicest perhaps among the drop-leaf mahogany dining room tables, both of the four- and six-leg variety, are those of the Sheraton type with the round, reeded legs usually capped at the end with a brass cup caster. As a general thing it may be assumed that such tables were earlier than the other types mentioned above, Sheraton having successfully survived both Chippendale and Hepplewhite. The purely Sheraton table of the sort just mentioned was popular

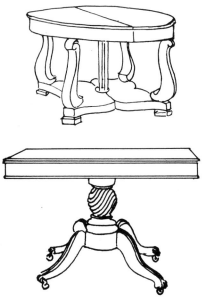

FIG. 59. (Upper) A massive mahogany veneered dining table with heavy scrolled legs of the 1840's. Obviously a John Hall creation of the extension type. (Lower) Empire dining table, 1825-30.

during the first quarter of the nineteenth century, but that should not be taken to mean that no such tables were made after 1825 or that their popularity among folk who could afford them came suddenly to an end in 1825.

More elegant dining tables, of the same period and perhaps more scarce, were produced with single and double pedestals, these being

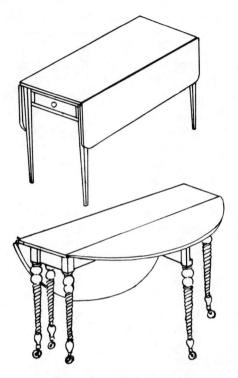

Fig. 60. (Upper) A widely used provincial table design of the early part of the nineteenth century. Although called a Hepplewhite table it owes nothing to that designer. The square tapered leg was simply a decorative device easy to achieve with hand tools. Many makers of such tables in the hinterlands had never heard of Hepplewhite. Some such tables were made in all cherry or all maple, some in combination of the two woods. (Lower) A formal mahogany gate-leg table of the late 1820's. Spiral turning on legs. Often called rope turning. Table belongs to Empire-Federal period but does not project either Empire or Federal motifs.

somewhat massive and deeply carved, usually with claw or claw-and-ball feet, four to the pedestal. A few such tables were also made with spiral reeding and what may be called Phyfe-type feet capped with brass at the ends, the feet being four in number and curving outward 90 degrees from the base of the pedestal.

Some of the single pedestal tables, of the larger and more elegant types and with heavily carved pedestals almost the diameter of a beer keg, were round when closed but long and commodious when opened at the center (draw) and provided with extra leaves. Most were done in mahogany. Indeed this was the great era of mahogany, an era that was not to close until after the first five years of the beginning of the Queen's reign when for some reason or other, perhaps because of the availability of the wood, walnut came into vogue with rosewood running a close second. Naturally the use of mahogany added considerable expense to any article of furniture because the wood had to be imported. During the 1840's farmers in all parts of the country cut and sold their walnut trees at relatively high prices.

The rural folk during the first half of the nineteenth century could not usually afford anything but a table that simply filled a need. Thousands upon thousands of homemade tables, some of them unbelievably crude, were produced during these times and with nothing much by way of design by which they could now be classified. Few have come down to the present time largely because of unskilled workmanship and because many of them were of pine. This wood was favored by the home craftsman because of the ease with which an unskilled person could fashion it, but shunned by the professional joiner because it did not have the strength required for such things as tables, chairs or beds; a good wood but not a strong one. The pine chests and cupboards were different matters; they were furniture that was not required to bear up under strain and furniture without long legs which, through the action of leverage, brought great force to bear upon mortised joints. Some of the early and more heavy gate-leg tables of the 1750's and later were of pine but few of them have for this reason survived to the present day, whereas those produced from oak are still among the hale and hearty survivors after two hundred years.

When the early nineteenth century farmers and other rural folk, among them the tanners, the candlemakers, the cobblers, the tinsmiths, the harnessmakers, the coopers, and the millers, could afford to employ a joiner, they gained possession of tables that were able

FIG. 61. A single pedestal Empire dining table of heavily carved mahogany. *Circa* 1830. (Courtesy Mrs. George Carnochan)

to bear up under great abuse. Here and there a pine top might be found on such a table but rarely pine legs or frames.

In the years between 1820 and 1845 (roughly, that is) such dining and other tables, especially bedside stands, were made of local wild cherry, maple, or a combination of both, with the table frames and tops of cherry and the legs of maple which was rarely clear. Usually it bore a stripe or a burl and the legs were usually square and tapered in the Hepplewhite manner rather than round. Not all joiners had lathe benches and besides maple in burl was tough stuff to turn unless one had a turning machine driven by a horse treadmill or with water power.

Some of these dining tables were four-leg drop-leafs and some were six-leg gate types. They were equally produced but present demand has raised the price for the six-leg tables out of all proportion to that asked for the four-leg types. So true is this that the beginner is warned to watch for reproductions of the former. These tables (the six-leg gate-leg) now command anywhere from $150 to $250 each. Because of their simplicity, they offer a great temptation to tinkers with maple and cherry at hand. Given the wood and modern wood-working machinery, such a table could be produced for a few dollars and sold to some unsuspecting victim (as has been done in supposedly reliable shops!) at a five hundred per cent profit.

Fortunately detection of such frauds is not too difficult, although exposure to ammonia fumes or ammonia liquid can give an acceptable old patina to cherry. For one thing, a purchaser should be very suspicious of freshly smeared glue at the joints; that is where the side and end frame boards are mortised into the tops of the legs. Such table frames were also made of thick pieces of cherry board, never under and more often well over one inch in thickness.

The tops and leaves on reproduced tables are often dead giveaways. During the early and mid-nineteenth century in this country when these tables were in vogue, there were a great many wild cherry trees of great girth, a girth so great indeed that the old joiners could take twenty-four-inch boards from them. Hence only rarely did they butt cherry boards and glue them together for table tops and leaves. One has reason indeed to question the authenticity of such a table leaf or top made up of two, three, or more pieces.

In the legitimate restoration of such tables, badly warped tops and leaves are often sawed in lengths and glued back together, which provides a rippled surface in place of a sweeping, single warp. This done, the tops or leaves are then run through a planing machine which takes the ripples out but leaves the assembled board rather thin, as might be expected in view of the fact that the board is run through the planer first on one side and then on the other. The old

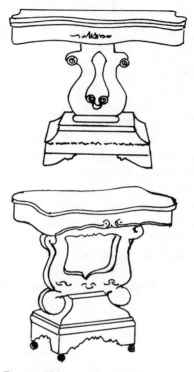

Fig. 62. Two console tables from the 1850's. Characterized by massive, scrolled pedestals, with crotch mahogany veneering. Such tables were extremely popular well into the 1860's.

table tops were usually more than one inch thick and hence can take such treatment if one wishes to carry restoration that far in the interest of appearance. There, however, the unscrupulous merchant of spurious wares has an "out." He can say that his reproduction has been through such a process. Fortunately there are other reliable marks of age.

The tops of such tables (old tops, that is) were held to the frame from beneath by the use of blunt-end screws, and good restoration, if it has to be resorted to at all (many people rightly prize a slight warp to such tables as a mark of age), requires that the old screws be replaced. Therefore new screws may present another cause for suspicion.

The cherry, walnut, or maple boards used in the frames of these old tables were dressed without benefit of planers, this being handwork with a hollow plane that left recognizable marks in the form of slight undulations in the surfaces of the boards. Running the finger tips lightly over the surfaces of these boards will reveal this imperfection; the argument of the dealer that the boards were also planed over is not valid. There is no need of taking these table frames apart and reworking them.

These data relating to fraud have been included because of the traffic in this sort of reproduction during the past few years. Just a few months before the present work went to press, many hundreds of reproduction six-leg tables in cherry were released into the western New York market, most of them sold as originals. Such a reproduction might legitimately be worth one hundred dollars. An original would be worth one hundred dollars more, and many of the dealers who purchased these reproductions could not resist the temptation to make the additional profit. This was not, unfortunately, an isolated instance with regards to either cherry or walnut tables of the variety used between 1845 and 1875. It is the case of an extremely popular item that is easy to make with modern machinery, and later tables of this type were indeed made with machinery. Another mark of the reproduced table or the table that has been restored beyond all reason, with perhaps nothing original left but its frame, is the exceptionally wide drop leaf coming within a few inches of the floor. Few if any of the original tables of this type had such wide leaves.

In the case of the later types of factory-made gate-leg tables, the simple tests and observations needed to detect fraud are not useful. Such tables were made with smooth boards, glue, the new type of gimlet screws, etc. These were the tables of the 1840's and later (to 1875) with turned legs, etc. They were immensely popular with rural folk and lower-middle-class urban people during the years mentioned and were produced in furniture factories in great numbers; indeed, they were mass-produced, the legs being turned with special cutting tools by the hundreds of thousands in walnut, cherry, and maple. Some legs were plain and tapered with Sheraton feeling,

FIG. 63. An Early Victorian table made probably not later than 1845 and representing a general style that remained popular well into the 1860's. (Courtesy Florence E. Wright)

some were button-turned, and some had ball turning, both of the latter now loosely called "spool" by people not familiar with proper terminology.

Four-leg drop-leaf tables of the same sort were also made at the same time but in lesser numbers. A catalogue published in the late 1860's and now in the hands of the writers shows the price of a cherry six-leg table with ball turnings to have been eight dollars.

That is about one hundred and ninety-two dollars less than the price asked a short time ago when the popularity of such near-antiques was at its peak.

After the break with American Empire in the early 1840's, formal, expensive dining room tables in mahogany or walnut reached pretty low levels artistically speaking. One can have a fair word for some

FIG. 64. A more dainty form of the Mid-Victorian console table with crotch mahogany veneer and piecrust molding. *Circa* 1850's. (Owned by Mrs. George Carnochan, Lewiston, N. Y.)

of the chairs and chests of the 1840's but for the pompous dining tables used by the swells, never.

Card and game tables were very popular during the first half of the nineteenth century. Almost all of the earlier tables of this sort were in mahogany and practically all had carved legs, when they were not Hepplewhite in styling. Occasionally one comes across such a table (usually Hepplewhite) in striped or burled maple, the Hepplewhite leg being suitable for this wood, which could not easily be carved because of grain structure.

What has been said concerning the game or card table may also be said about console tables. Some of them were of the pedestal type, some had four legs. Some were Hepplewhite, some Sheraton, and some in the styles that had been set by Duncan Phyfe. All small tables of the formal types, including the worktables or sewing tables and the bedside tables, followed pretty much along the lines outlined above.

FIG. 65. A marble top table of the late 1880's with a distinct Eastlake flavor. (Courtesy Miss Florence E. Wright)

To the above list might also be added the less popular sofa table of which Duncan Phyfe is known to have produced a fair number. Apparently, like many other furniture customs and styles this innovation had been imported from England. The sofa table was relatively long and obviously intended to be placed behind a sofa.

All of the tables just mentioned are expensive, all represent the approaching end of good furniture design in America. The blight that was to continue to the present time began to set in in the 1830's or sooner with the appearance of the later forms of American Empire, which a friend of one of the writers once very aptly called "bloated Sheraton." Granted that French Empire (1804) reflected the pomposity of a dictator who had always been too conscious of his own small stature. Yet with all of its shortcomings there was a certain dignity to the pieces and they virtually exuded neoclassicism: Roman, Grecian, and Egyptian.

Although Hall tables were by no means as plentiful as the later types of oval marble-topped tables in walnut, diligent search may discover a true Hall console or center table with heavy scrolled pedestal and black marble top, made perhaps before the apparently insatiable demand for walnut developed in the latter part of the 1840's. Hall rarely appeared in walnut dress.

Apparently the popularity of the oval, square, and oblong marble-topped tables in walnut continued to grow between 1845 and the 1870's and early 1880's, the last ten years of the vogue producing some of the most awkward monstrosities of all time. They were machine-carved in heaven only knows what fashion, but a fashion to produce prolonged seizures of artistic dyspepsia in anyone with even half an eye for beauty in any form. The least damnable of these tables were produced between the years 1850 and 1865 or 1870; but Eastlake had corrupted them as he did everything that he influenced. Those who like such tables in the more sober moods (though still pretty terrible!) may wish to search for one in mahogany done between the years 1850 and 1865. They are much less easy to find than the walnut tables.

It is too much to expect authors dealing with Victorian antiques to suffer the punishment of exploring the Eastlake era and its tables or any furniture belonging to that horrible period of debauched taste.

CHAPTER VI

What the Victorians Slept On

FOR those who would have Victorian bedrooms complete from commode to towelrack, the bed presents a problem. For some reason beds made during these years are not in good supply, many dealers either refusing to handle them or, except for the largest dealers, having a small stock.

Pre-Victorian beds (say between 1800 and 1835), except the primitives, are not only in very small supply but very expensive. Why this is so is not known since most families were large and many houses had a number of sleeping chambers.

The tester or canopy beds invaded the nineteenth century up to as late as the 1840's; in Sheraton, Hepplewhite, and Empire, both Early and Late, and it was not unusual to find them in use as late as in Civil War times. Some testers had plain posts turned from maple or cherry, some were of elaborately carved mahogany. Some may be had today for as little as one hundred dollars, some for nothing less than one thousand dollars. If one wishes to indulge in Sheraton or Chippendale beds, even those traceable to the early nineteenth century, the pocketbook must be amply padded. Strictly speaking, of course, such beds are not Victorian unless one wishes to stretch the length of the Queen's period to include her birth in 1819. Duncan Phyfe, too, made a few four-posters during the early part of the nineteenth century while he was at his best as a designer, but acquiring such things can take form only in the dreams of most collectors. They are very rare, very costly.

It is not to be denied that at least a few four-poster beds with canopies were made during the Victorian period. They were pro-

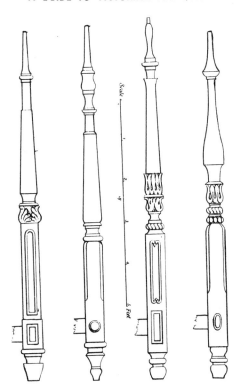

FIG. 66. Posts for Victorian canopy or tester beds suggested by the Baltimore architect, John Hall, in his book of furniture design published in 1840.

duced during the first years of the Queen's reign. However, they were the final result of the transition period that set in during the very early 1820's. Up to that time canopy or tester beds had posts relatively small in diameter, those of Sheraton type being turned from the frame up in elongated vase form, the foot portion being of larger diameter and also of vase form. Such beds were graceful and charming but soon the badly proportioned, massive forms of the later version of American Empire began to rob such beds of their beauty. The posts became larger—much larger—in diameter and a penchant for deep carving took possession of the joiners' craft. It was then that the eventually overdone acanthus leaf motif began to appear, a vogue that stretched over a period that almost, if not quite, touched the vogue established by John Hall of Baltimore, who brought forth his new book in 1840. Those beds with their massive square rails and legs could have supported Barnum's Jumbo without so much as a grunt or a squeak.

Not all of these Late Empire beds, however, were of the canopy type. Some, also called four-posters, had short posts, and some had posts of medium height without canopies. Not a few such beds were imported into this country from the West Indies, but only the experts who know the homelands of the various mahogany woods and the finer subtleties of workmanship can distinguish between these beds and the American product. In so far as the average collector is concerned the difference is not important. As to beauty, they were questionable; but as to workmanship, let no man say that these beds owed much to the immortals of the eighteenth century. God did not reserve the last half of the eighteenth century exclusively for skilled wood-carvers; Nutting, Ormsbee, or Drepperd notwithstanding.

Usually it was only the better homes that had the four-poster canopy or tester bed in any form, hence their relative scarcity. Lesser folk had to be satisfied with the more ordinary, low four-poster bed without benefit (if it was a benefit) of a canopy covering. Such beds continued to be made during the whole first half of the nineteenth century and are therefore very common and relatively cheap. Most of the earlier ones are either single or three-quarters in size. The three-quarter bed suggests the necessity for mutual cuddling during the days when draughty homes were heated by few fireplaces, whose fire usually expired long before the cocks crowed or the cows mooed for their morning feeding.

Little wonder, though, that these beds that have come down to us by the thousands, lived to see the days when ladies accustomed to television and hundred-mile-an-hour motor cars bid them in at country auctions for a few dollars. They were simply but marvelously made, with rails rarely less than four inches square or four inches in diameter (when round) and with legs that would have supported tons of weight. Rare it is, indeed, to find such beds needing extensive repair or even so much as a tap from a hammer or a stroke of the saw, except in making them adaptable to modern mattresses. The sides and bottom rails were either drilled or provided with knobs to accommodate the woven rope that supported the old feather mattresses.

It is rare, indeed, to find such beds made in mahogany, although here and there a lower-middle-class family indulged in such luxury. Such beds usually appear in cherry or maple; less commonly by far in pine or walnut. The head- and footboards were scrolled and had projections mortised into the posts. Some had only scrolled headboards and no footboards.

One occasionally comes across these beds decorated with stencil designs and equipped with a baluster at the foot which served as a blanket roll, the baluster being free to turn in the bearings provided by the foot posts; but such beds are not common. Occasionally the stencilling included Masonic emblems. In any event these beds are assigned to the Late Empire period when heavy chests were also decorated with stencils on their drawer fronts. Such a chest and such a bed along with a fancy chair, a fancy Boston rocker, a clock having stencilled pilasters, and a mirror with the same thing will provide the collector with an 1825 bedroom perfect in every detail and something fondly to be admired.

The earliest (nineteenth century, that is) of these low four-poster beds followed pretty much the same pattern, variation in design being pretty much limited to turnings. Come the 1830's, there was more expression of individuality, some downright experimentation with new forms. Posts began to appear with ball, mushroom, acorn, and bell tops, and tops that resembled nothing in particular. Occasionally one finds the top coming to a point. However this variation in production is not to be wondered at when it is known that perhaps as many as twenty thousand men were engaged in making

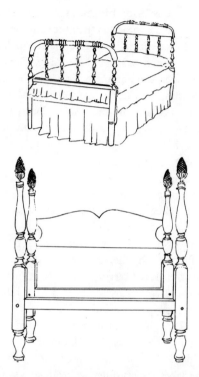

Fig. 67. (Upper) Turned spindle bedstead with vase motif. Some are also found with turned ball and lemon shape. Erroneously called a spool bed. Factory-made in large numbers during the 1850's. (Lower) Late Empire bed in mahogany with pineapple finials. This type of bed is very much in demand and commands high prices. Probably made as early as 1825 and as late as 1840.

furniture, not in factories but in their little turning and joinery shops.

By the 1840's the beds made by the independents whom competition had not yet driven into the furniture factories were on the whole pretty bad. Some old fellows, due mostly to habit, continued to make their beds much as they had made them twenty years before, but they were in the minority. This was the era that brought forth that curious thing called the spool bed. Although the writers have visited hundreds of antique shops in various parts of the country and have read so many books devoted to antiques as to make Dr. Eliot's famous Five-Foot bookshelf five feet too short, never once have they seen a spool bed or a picture of one. When such things are pointed out to the writers, the "pointer-outers" must finally admit that either a form of ball turning or lemon turning is involved. Most so-called spool beds, however, are factory-made products of the engine-driven lathes, the owners of which wanted to "turn hell out of everything," as a friend once put it. It has to be admitted that some of the earlier beds of this type are now "under the wire" and into the sacred territory of the antique. Unfortunately these beds were made for many years and in a number of forms, cursed as they are to strip and refinish.

And the Jenny Jind bed? That depends upon the imagination, gullibility, and ignorance of the lady looking for such a thing, to say nothing of "dealers" who know little more than she and who are quick to put a label on anything to produce a sale.

Although the carved four-posters in mahogany were popular in the 1830's, they did not wholly dominate the field of better-class beds in this wood. One of the present writers rests very comfortably on an Empire bed that goes back to early French sources for its inspiration and may be said to be more truly Empire than the four-posters of carved mahogany. It is what the ladies nowadays call a sleigh bed. Some call it a scroll bed but it is really a more or less faithful model of the bed in which the great Corporal of France slept at his Trianon palace in the heyday of his career. It is minus the gold decorations of the original piece but still much like it in

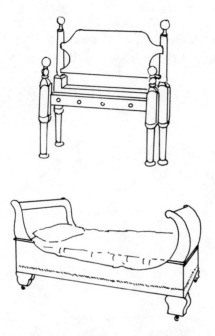

Fig. 68. (Upper) Simple type of country-made bed in maple. Some were in
cherry and (less frequently) in walnut.
Some had foot-boards, some did not.
Finials varied a great deal, although most
of either bell, ball, or mushroom shape.
The one common characteristic of these
beds was massiveness. In various types
and forms they were produced from the
very early part of the nineteenth century
up to the 1860's. (Lower) The scroll
Empire bed copied after Napoleon's bed
at Trianon. Often called a sleigh bed.
Covered with crotch mahogany with the
later forms (1840's) decorated with machine-cut piecrust molding.

general outline. These beds were made in America during the years between 1835 and 1845 and were more popular in the South than in the North.

Due to an invention by one John Hewitt, a New York cabinet-maker, later beds of this type are found wherein the side boards or

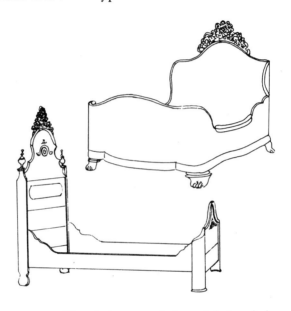

Fig. 69. (Upper) A rosewood plywood bed made by John Belter of New York City during the mid-1850's. (Lower) An example of the gawky type of walnut bed made during the 1870's. Such beds usually had exceptionally high headboards.

rails are attached to the head- and footboards by means of a hooked iron catch still employed to this very day. Earlier types used heavy iron screws with square heads.

Such beds were covered with fine veneer and more often than not later types were decorated very modestly with piecrust molding which was machine-cut. Used with the better-class mahogany chests of the same era and a mahogany chair and bedside table of the same period, these beds may be the centerpieces of bedrooms not too wanting in acceptable taste. Such beds bring one hundred dollars or less, depending upon the part of the country in which they are purchased. They are not rare.

On the whole the Americans did not copy French Empire with any great degree of fidelity and the French Empire vogue occurred

FIG. 70. This knobby, carved-up monstrosity plastered with crotch walnut veneering was made especially for the Mr. Moneybags of the 1870's. Hideous in the extreme, yet already a candidate for antiquity.

much earlier (1805-1810) than the time the scroll bed became popular in this country. How curious that this belated revival of a truly French Empire bed should have appeared in the 1830's and should have been more truly French than any of the pieces that had been made during the early American vogue for Napoleon's pomposity.

Many and varied were the types of beds both elegant and common that came forth from the furniture factories between the years

1850 and 1890. To add to the confusion, not a few of the independent cabinetmakers produced individual beds until perhaps as late as 1870. Not the least among these was Belter of New York City, although very few of his beds remain and it would be most unusual to find one in a shop. It was in his beds that Belter first used his laminated five-ply rosewood. Today it would be called plywood. Belter patented the idea in 1854. On the whole Belter beds were not too bad, most of them being far less ornate and overly carved than his chairs and tables.

During the 1860's, the massive, awkward walnut beds came into vogue. They were characterized not only by their general ugliness but also by their exceptionally high headboards. The final corruption settled upon these hapless pieces of furniture after 1870, when Charles Eastlake became the vogue of American homeowners. However, the beds of the 1860's had been so ably spoiled from an artistic viewpoint that Eastlake's influence did not worsen it as much as it might otherwise have done.

Before this chapter comes to a close, a note on the so-called trundle bed might be useful, especially in view of the fact that many people think that such beds were used only in Pilgrim times. They were, in fact, used in rural America up to the 1860's, the decade of the 1860's probably bringing to a close a hundred years or more of their very useful career. It was the trundle bed with its very stubby legs and castors that was rolled away under the ordinary bed when not in use for the unexpected guest or for the child or children for whom a new room had not yet been added to the farmstead. Trundle beds have never been popular with antique collectors.

CHAPTER VII

Lamps and Lighting

AS IN the case of many other things that belong to the era of the Queen's reign, a number of the provincial lighting fixtures used during the first half of the nineteenth century are erroneously given a much earlier existence and this, as often as not, by people who should know better. The so-called betty lamp or "grease lamp" is a case in point. It is very difficult to refute the belief that this lamp was an exclusively Pilgrim invention (it was brought over from England) or that the use of the thing continued beyond the 1750's (as a matter of fact, many of the farmers of the Midwest used such lamps until the 1860's). The type was no doubt different but it was still a betty lamp. Betty lamps very similar to those made in New England in the early 1700's were produced in Ohio during the 1830's and 1840's.

Doubtless the poorest among the poor of early America used the rushlight; even the very poor Victorian provincials may have used it. This rush lamp was simply a rush blossom soaked in fat or oil. After all, the need for a night light was short in those days. There were no detective stories to be read, no twelve o'clock newscasts to wait for. Of course, the betty lamp with no change in principle and very little change in design came down from the early Romans. The arrangement was simple enough: a cotton or other cloth wick dipping into a container of animal fat, its outside end being lit and the wick carrying the oil to the flame by capillary attraction.

The drawing showing the early lamp types and forms will illustrate the small differences between the seventeenth century and nineteenth century betty lamps.

135

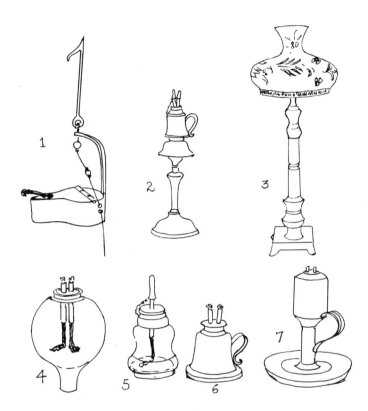

FIG. 71. (1) An eighteenth century betty lamp with jam hook and pickwick. (2) Pewter lamp in candleholder form of the 1830's. (3) The true form of the astral-solar lamps as used in this country and England during the early part of the nineteenth century. Usually without prisms. (4) Peg lamps in glass intended for use in candleholder. Peg lamps also appeared in pewter and tin. (5) Small glass whale oil lamps, single burner, of the 1840's. (6) Pewter lamp of the 1830's. (7) Tin whale oil lamp of the 1830's. A wide variety of such lamps were made by village tinsmiths between the years 1820 and 1860.

There was also to be considered the so-called Phoebe lamp, but this, too, was a grease or fat burner and not nearly so widespread in use as the betty lamp, which appeared first in ancient times in pottery, then in cast iron, then in tin, the latter used both in Late Colonial times and during the first half of the nineteenth century, when such lamps were fashioned in a wide variety of forms and improvement by village tinsmiths. Potters in various parts of the country, especially in Pennsylvania, also made such lamps.

Let those who doubt that a form of the betty lamp lived into the second half of the nineteenth century, turn to the patent issued to one Zuriel Swope of Lancaster, Pennsylvania, on March 13, 1860. This patent covered improvements in crude lard oil lamps and such lamps were doubtless used in the United States until the 1870's. It was then part of a farmer's secure and independent life that he was able to supply his own illuminant.

Although the provincials used lard oil for many years, the townspeople took to whale oil during the early part of the nineteenth century. It was better, cleaner, less odoriferous and sooty. Special lamps were devised of glass, tin, or pewter to burn this oil. Both the Sandwich Glass Company and the New England Glass Works produced the chimney-less lamps of pressed glass during the late 1820's; lamps that are now so keenly sought after and which represent nineteenth century flint glass at its best.

Such lamps were simple enough, being only a font of glass pressed, fused integrally with the pedestal, and having (after 1830) a threaded pewter ring on the top into which the burner was placed. This burner consisted only of two tin tubes soldered to a circular member that passed through a button-like disk threaded to match the pewter ring cemented to the top opening of the font. The circular cotton wicks passed through the tin tubes. There were no knurled wheels with which to turn a wick up or down, no way indeed to prevent the formation of soot or odor from the open flames.

Yet such lamps were considered great luxuries in their day not because of original cost but because of the cost of maintenance, what with whale oil at thirty-five cents a gallon. Sperm oil, so called

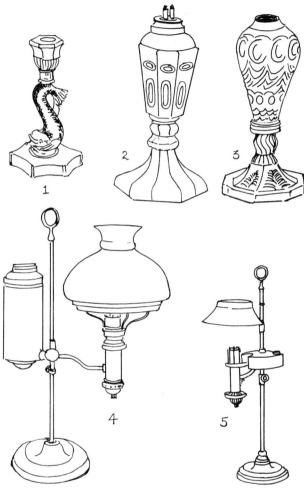

FIG. 72. (1) Sandwich glass dolphin candle holder. Made in various colors. Pittsburgh also produced such holders in great numbers and in many colors. Principal difference between the two products is in base. (2 and 3) Pressed Sandwich whale lamps of the 1840's. (4) The single student lamp of the 1880's. (5) The grandaddy of the student lamp and in all probability its inspiration: the Argand lamp of 1800.

because it was taken from the head of the sperm whale and which could also be used in such lamps, was a superior illuminant but cost nearly one dollar a gallon. The use of these oils and the preparation known as camphene went along until the advent of kerosene, or "coal oil" as it was first known. The introduction of this oil and of the flat cotton wick during the early 1860's spelled doom not only for the whaling industry but for all other oil preparations, such as Porter's Fluid, camphene, etc.

J. Porter, of Boston, developed an illuminant by treating oil of turpentine with quicklime, apparently to remove the rosin and eliminate the troublesome smoke caused by this ingredient. Camphene, another illuminant of the time, was a mixture of treated turpentine and alcohol. This fluid provoked both threats and warnings by the fire insurance companies, and with great justification due to the large number of explosions and fires involving the special lamps. Patented burners were devised to prevent the accumulation of dangerous heat in the lamp reservoirs and these were moderately successful.

Choicest among the early nineteenth century lamps are the blown-and-molded types produced between 1826 and 1840 by the Sandwich Glass Company and the New England Glass Works. These were intended for the burning of whale oil and were made with a threaded pewter collar into which the piece holding two metal wick tubes was fitted. The reservoirs were blown into a pattern mold and then welded while hot to the pressed glass base or pedestal. Examples of such lamps are also found in which no molding was used, the base being hand formed.

The first of such lamps were quite small but they grew both in size and beauty, many exquisite types being brought out in the 1830's. Especially sought and especially rare are those of later Sandwich manufacture with either dolphin or lacy bases.

Doubtless the most beautiful of the whale oil lamps were produced by molding alone, the clear ones being made in the Bull's Eye, Sweetheart, Fleur de Lys, and Diamond patterns, to list a few of the more relatively common varieties. Such lamps were rarely more than ten inches high or less than eight. As collectors' items they are in the category of diamonds, in that one can be assured that the price will never go down.

And then, of course, there are the so-called sparking lamps, embracing so far as these writers are concerned a bit of tradition that is pure nonsense. These were very small whale or sperm oil lamps of blown and pressed glass, perhaps more of the blown, by far, than of the pressed. Apparently they began to appear on the American scene about the time the Sandwich Glass Company started production (1826). The fonts, being small, held little oil and consequently the light had but a short life. Watchful fathers were said to have insisted on such lights when the beaver-hatted swains called on their daughters. The hard facts of the case do not have so romantic a quality. Whale and sperm oil were expensive and not even the best lamps intended for parlor illumination had large capacities. Even the larger lamps are sometimes called sparking lamps by the more romantic ladies among present collectors of Victorian Americana.

Among the rarest and choicest of the so-called sparking lamps are the very early wineglass types. Being made of thin glass, they naturally did not survive the years as well as some of their more robust contemporaries. The wineglass types are all in clear glass and have only rudimentary decorations if they have any at all.

It would be quite impossible to list all of the early lamp patterns or varieties here. Although in general it may be said that the very short ones (six inches high or less) with plain reservoirs or fonts are apt to be among the very early types, the reservoir being fused to the molded base. Later ones were not only taller but on the whole heavier, especially the reservoir although it was relatively small, a fact that suggests early bedtime hours among Americans during the first half of the nineteenth century. On the whole it might be said of such lamps that they were long and lean and heavy in weight. They had globes but not chimneys, the latter being an addition that did not come until the 1850's.

Choice as the early clear-glass lamps of this type are, those made in colored glass are better and far more rare; collectible items all.

Even the haughtiest of the connoisseurs do not look down their noses at them—much. Some were in milk-white glass (not a color really), some in blue, some in yellow and amethyst, with waffle and block patterns. If Grandma still has one of these, one can afford to be nice to Grandma!

In discussing these early lamps one must also include the early peg lamps. Only the more well-fixed of the American families could afford to burn whale oil, the sort of family that might have nice Sheffield or silver candlesticks about the house. Naturally such people did not wish suddenly to discard such choice things. Sandwich and others accommodated these folk with a peg lamp, which had a font with a glass peg at the bottom that would slip into the candle hole of a candlestick. Not to be outdone by the city people, the country tinkers who worked in tin also made such things for their trade; in tin, of course. The pewterers, too, made pewter lamps of the same kind, and rare they are today. Not only did the tinners and the pewterers make such peg lamps but they also made the complete whale-oil lamp as a counterpart of the glass specimens referred to.

Some people insist on calling many of the lamps of the late 1850's and 1860's peg lamps, which stretches the meaning of the term. True, the glass reservoirs of such lamps were provided with a peg of glass or a protrusion often equipped with threads which matched the threads of a brass ferrule attached to the top of the lamp standard or column. In any case, the peg was not seen after the lamp was assembled. In the case of the plain peg, litharge cement was used to make the union between the lamp and the supporting column.

These 1850–60 lamps, although in no sense rare except in a few cases where color and overlay is involved, are now just approaching the age required of an antique and are among good collectibles. The bowls or reservoirs are sometimes plain, sometimes have variations of the ribbed or thumb print pattern with the reservoir tending more to the bulbous shape. Some stems were brass, the foot being a square slab of dressed marble. Others were of glass, many being milk-white. Delectable specimens of such lamps also appear with exquisite overlay. They are not too rare although they command heavy prices. However, the purchaser is on pretty safe ground from an investment viewpoint provided he does not pay too much. Such things were also made during the early 1870's although these years began to bring the ugly marks of deterioration, not only in lamps but in all things. They were indeed the years of transition.

During the 1850's the so-called Venetian lamp enjoyed a brief but

FIG. 73. (Left) Cast brass candelabra of the 1840's and (right) brass Venetian lamp for use with sperm oil. Imported from Italy during 1840's and 1850's. Equipped with pickwick, snuffer, and trimming shears.

not extensive popularity. This was a cast brass lamp with a font that was held by a small brass column and which was supplied with a number of spouts through which the wicks protruded. A pickwick, scissors, and a snuffer hung from the standard at the end of a small brass chain. Most if not all of these lamps were imported from Italy.

The Argand burner was a distinctly superior device and was used by the wealthy English for many years before it became popular over here. A few such lamps were imported into the States during the early part of the nineteenth century. It was not until the 1830's,

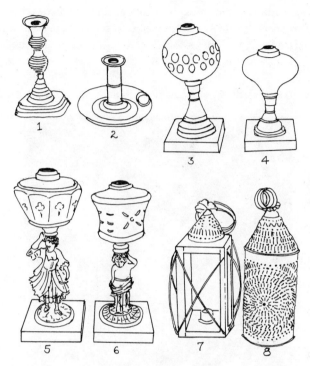

FIG. 74. (1) Formal brass candleholder imported from England during 1820's. (2) Simple brass holder used between the years 1815 and 1860. (3 and 4) Types of kerosene or coal oil lamps of the early 1860's. (5 and 6) Romantic lamps of the 1870's with cast white metal supports in human form. (7) A barn candle lantern of the type used generally between the years 1815 and 1870. (8) Glassless barn lantern of pierced tin, made by local tinsmiths and used well into the 1860's.

however, that it began to be produced here, in Philadelphia, and then in the form of what was known as a mantel lamp, usually sold in pairs, one for each side of the mantel mirror. The photograph shows one of the types, without prisms or crystals, in which oil is fed by gravity from a glass or brass reservoir mounted above the burners, the latter covered with a frosted globe. A few had glass bases, but most were in brass. Such things are expensive today, but they were in use throughout the 1840's. In terms of the depreciated dollar of today, these lamps sold for about two hundred dollars a pair in 1835, a figure not far from what one might expect to pay today.

There is considerable looseness of terminology in connection with

Fig. 75. (Left) Mantle lamp in brass. Argand variety produced during the 1840's. (Right) Astral type lamp also made during the 1840's. (Courtesy Olde Lamps, Inc., Buffalo, N. Y.)

the astral lamp. Some call the mantel lamp an astral when really it is but a contemporary of the astral. The type most commonly referred to as astral is a lamp with a brass column (usually reeded), a marble base, a brass reservoir with a shade ring mounted around it, a frosted glass shade in tulip or other design, and prisms hanging from the shade rim. A few such lamps were rather squat with short columns but most were fourteen to sixteen inches tall. The acceptance of such lamps as true astrals is a mistake in a strict sense, but

144

they may certainly be regarded as astral types or first cousins of the true astral, which is pictured herewith.

The astral type of lamp persisted for many years, from the 1830's into the 1860's, some of the late ones having been manufactured for burning kerosene, or coal oil. Perhaps the true astral was intended for reading because many were without prisms which would have cast shadows.

Fɪɢ. 76. Pressed-glass girandole, Late Victorian, but of a general type used during Early Victorian times.

The candleholder and candelabrum, both in fancy and in humble forms, survived all of these improvements in lighting. Even today some countryfolk in New England go upstairs with such things and by courtesy of the oil companies. All of the silversmiths and silverware concerns of the periods being discussed kept on making candleholders in various forms as did the makers of glass, pewter, brass, and Sheffield articles. The girandoles in beautiful glass were most popular in the 1840's, as were the glass candelabra for the wellappointed dining rooms. One may also find, as of the 1860's or later, lovely glass girandoles with prisms intended for the mantel. These are still desirable collectibles worthy of note. Nor should the collectors forget the much-sought-after pressed-glass candleholders in Dolphin and other designs. These appeared in great numbers during the 1860's, although they had been introduced many years before by Sandwich. Some were in clear glass, some in colored glass. The point to be remembered by the beginning collector is that come the 1860's, Dolphin candlesticks were made by a number of concerns,

Fig. 77. Miniature or bedside lamps of the 1870's and 1880's. Hundreds of different designs were produced.

notably among them McKee and Brothers of Pittsburgh, Pennsylvania, who sold them wholesale for $6.75 a dozen. These had circular bases while those produced by Sandwich were scalloped. Smaller concerns did not bother to make such a distinction between their own product and that produced by Sandwich. Therefore the beginner is warned to use discretion when asked to purchase a pair of Sandwich Dolphins in any color.

The appearance of kerosene or coal oil in the early 1860's brought corruption to the lamp. Colonel Drake did for lamps what Eastlake and the newer forms of woodworking machinery did for furniture ten years later. Kerosene was a cheap illuminant that most city folk and a lot of country folk could afford to use. A mighty, new market for lamps was opened almost overnight, and the production machinery owned by a crew of business men without art set about satisfying this market with all manner of monstrosities. Lamps became uglier and uglier as a few types shown will indicate. Here and there were manufacturers who produced lamps with some feeling for form and color but they were much in the minority.

Fig. 78. Examples of the Fairy lamp introduced into this country at the Chicago World's Fair in 1893 by its English inventor, Clarke. (From collection of Mrs. Penn Perkins, Molyneaux Corners, N. Y.)

Some of the little bedside or sick room lamps made between 1870 and 1890 were exceptions to the general rule, tiny and daintily painted with flowers as some of the better types were. Colored glass lamps of this sort, and lamps in Sandwich type glass in blue, milk, and other colors are among the best and rarest. Such things in general were made by the hundreds of thousands and yet today they demand prices that, on the whole, are ridiculously high. These high prices will remain until the fad for collecting such lamps goes the way of all fads.

Also to be mentioned as belonging to the era of the miniature or bedside lamp which really replaced the candle, is the fairy lamp which had little more than decorative employment. This was in truth not a lamp at all but rather a fancy candleholder in colored glass. They come in several pieces and were commonly made in peachblow, Burmese, Nailsea, satin, or other glass. After having been introduced at the World's Fair in 1893 as an English idea, such "lamps" became popular in this country, although it was not the sort of popularity enjoyed by the miniature kerosene lamps, which resulted in a great number of hand-me-downs. The fairy lamp

FIG. 79. A fancy bracket lamp with frosted shade made during the early 1890's.

bowed itself in and out of the American scene within a few years whereas the miniature lamp held its position for forty-odd years. Fairy lamps are rather difficult to find in the average run of antique shops and they are expensive. In no sense can they be called antiques.

The miniature lamp was soon (about 1875) followed by the bracket lamp, apparently intended for kitchen use if one is to judge it by its design. Here and there a fancy bracket lamp with frosted shade makes an appearance, but such things are on the whole difficult to find.

The common type swing arm bracket lamp with the bracket cast in iron and either painted or bronzed was produced by hundreds of thousands between 1875 and 1910. They were stupid, ugly things for the most part and their present popularity (and price!) is very difficult to understand.

FIG. 80. An elaborate and beautiful type of wedding lamp made in the 1860's. (Courtesy Mrs. George Carnochan, Lewiston, N. Y.)

Such, too, is the case for the larger of the all-glass lamps of the period, few worthy of the notice of collectors save perhaps as interesting bits of Americana. The usually decorative miniature hand lamp had much to recommend it as a collector's item, but not so the larger types of hand lamps. The miniatures in milk glass, of various pressed patterns, Peacock Eye, Cabbage Rose, Thousand Eye, hobnail, etc., are bound to grow more valuable with the years.

Whereas the lamps of the mid-1850's and 1860's were beautiful more often than not, the passing of the year 1870 began to bring general bankruptcy artistically speaking. Gone were the days that produced such pattern delights as Sawtooth, Diamond Point, Bull's Eye, Fleur de Lys, Ivy, Argus, Honeycomb, etc. It was during these days, too, that the now much-sought-after marriage lamp made its appearance, an example of which is illustrated in the photograph.

The later lamps (1870 and after) became more gaudy and ugly in every respect. China stems smeared with painted flowers began to appear in the late 70's, the fonts being made of pressed glass in most ordinary designs. Most fonts were of clear glass, a few colored.

Fig. 81. (1 and 2) Common oil lamps of the 1870's with pressed pattern glass fonts, painted china stems, and cast-iron bases. (3 and 4) Pressed all-glass lamps of the 1860's and 1870's.

Bases were invariably of enameled cast iron. The stems or standards were thick and awkward in appearance.

The reader is asked to understand that a thorough history of the many types of lamps produced between the years 1870 and 1910 would not only require years of research but a volume twice the present size. The best that the writers can do is to guide the reader away from the pure trash and at the same time provide him with an over-all picture emphasizing the types of lamps that appeared rather than the varieties of types.

The 1870's also brought in the cast metal (usually some alloy with a low melting point) lamp stem or standard. These lamps beautifully typify the romanticism of the latter part of the Mauve

Decade. Here is a young lady, supposedly beautiful, carrying the font on her shoulder. In another instance a handsome youth is engaged in the same pursuit.

The vases of such lamps were usually of some sort of slate while the fonts were on the whole rather acceptable as the drawing of this sort of lamp will show.

Fig. 82. A three-piece Dresden type china lamp from the 1870's.

There was also a tendency at the beginning of the 1870's to make lamps taller, and some of the china lamps of this type were not too badly done from a decorative viewpoint.

The student lamp in all probability had its origin in Germany in the early 1860's or late 1870's. The inspiration for such lamps is not difficult to trace if one will search out pictures of certain types of the Argand lamp produced around 1800. The student lamp also bears a distinct relationship to the mantel lamps of the 1830's and 1840's. The student lamp had (in the beginning, that is) only a fifteen-year popularity in this country, dating from 1875 to 1890.

While student lamps are a little too brassy to suit many people, there is no doubt about the intensity of their revival. Lamps that brought seven or eight dollars when new now bring as much as $200. On the whole, student lamps are limited in design variation, the principal difference being between the lamps with one burner and those with two. Price is governed largely by the degree of

FIG. 83. A brass font lamp with frosted globe made during the late 1890's.

ornamentation and the nature of the glass shades. Ordinary white or green shades are the most common. Colored glass shades of certain types may raise the price asked for any double student lamp by fully one hundred dollars. Among the rarer shades are found such delectable (to the admirers of student lamps, at least) things as the ribbed shade with spattered gold, the Cranberry Thumbprint or Hobnail, and the Blue Satin, to mention a few of the more desirable.

Among student lamp rarities is the lamp with the fancy cast brass font. The present writers have seen them listed for as much as $250, which is a bit high for something perhaps no more than sixty years old, of highly questionable art value, and with an original price that did not exceed $25.

A number of American colleges introduced these lamps into dormitories. The so-called Harvard student lamps were supposed to

Fig. 84. Scarce student lamp called the Harvard. It has a cast brass font and was made for this university by Tiffany and Company. (Courtesy Olde Lamps, Inc., Buffalo, N. Y.)

have been made especially for this college. This also had a very decorative oil font cast in brass and many such lamps bore the mark of Tiffany and Company. Today they are among the most eagerly sought of the student lamps, and it must be conceded that they are the choicest.

For the beginning collector, the student lamp offers a hazard except when one is dealing with scrupulous people. Not only are reproductions being widely made and widely sold as such in our department stores but there has also appeared excellent reproduction of student-lamp shades. The differences between such reproductions and the original ₃hades of the same type are in some cases so subtle that any amateur should think twice before trusting himself to distinguish between the two. The sprayed shade, too, presents a real problem to the amateur. Some of the new spraying techniques produce such excellent effects of color plus preserving the thinness of the shade (which is one of the identifying properties of the old shades) that many nonexperts have been taken in. After all, the price differential between a reproduction and an original can be very substantial.

That modern monstrosity among monstrosities in lighting equipment, the Gone-With-the-Wind lamp, was doubtless brought back into use by its appearance in Scarlett O'Hara's room shown in the moving picture *Gone With the Wind.* How historically accurate the picture was in showing such lamps, even later in Scarlett's life, is debatable but the fact remains that a great body of American women rushed for their own and other people's attics to haul out these horrible examples of the lamp manufacturer's craft. Doubtless the ladies in the native villages of South Africa and Borneo would have admired them also, so colorful were they. Antique dealers who had until that time ignored such attic trash suddenly jumped into their station wagons to begin a search that eventually unearthed some of the most heinous conceptions that ever disturbed the human mind. The flood was great but so was the number of the outstretched hands holding twenty- or fifty-dollar bills.

These lamps really did not become popular until the 1890's and they were made until the 1920's, apparently the youngest among the many things that in recent years have been wrongly placed in the category of antiques. Only rarely does a person with any feeling come upon an acceptable lamp of this type, preferably hand painted and done by a person with some degree of artistic talent and in colors that do not shout to the high heavens. These lamps were among the more individual and therefore more expensive of the Gone-With-the-Wind lamps.

The hanging lamp appeared earlier than the G.W.W., but on the whole it is no more acceptable to people with taste, whether it has a Hobnail Cranberry shade or a plain white one, conical in shape and smeared with a few brush strokes supposed to represent flowers.

FIG. 85. One of the more presentable type of the so-called Gone-with-the-Wind lamps with delicately hand-painted china font and globe.

Many are hideous things, fine contemporaries for the G.W.W. lamps. Those equipped with prisms or glass drops are no more desirable than those without, although the prices range accordingly. In the opinion of the writers, some fine day the antique business is going to find the hanging lamp on its way back to the attic where it should be permitted to rest for another hundred years, along with the G.W.W.

CHAPTER VIII

Clocks

THERE is something charming and in a way comforting about
an old Victorian or Pre-Victorian mantel clock or shelf clock
ticking away on the mantel. What is more, the wish for such a clock
may in most cases be satisfied for a few dollars because clocks were
among the things that the Mid-Victorian manufacturers produced
with a vengeance.

That the early clock business is a complicated and confusing one
to study is indicated by the fact that one hundred odd pages, normal
book size, are required merely to list early American clockmakers,
most of them active between 1800 and 1850 in which period it
is assumed that the reader is chiefly interested. Not only that, but
the early manufacturers of clocks between 1820 and 1835 represented a shifting scene, companies often forming and dissolving
after a few months of operation and partnerships being established
and broken with amazing rapidity. After Terry opened the cheap
clock market in the early 1820's with his mass-produced wooden
works and made himself a considerable amount of money, the rush
to invade the business became a stampede. As soon as partnerships
turned out to be successful, either one or both of the partners wondered why he was silly enough to divide profits with the other.
Terry himself was in business with half a dozen men.

Most beginning collectors of antiques share the notion that clocks
with wooden works go back to the Year One. All of the early
clocks of Europe made during the seventeenth and eighteenth centuries were of brass, iron, steel, or copper and so it was in this
country, as late as sometime in the 1790's when some experimental

tinkering was done with wooden works. This was not, however, because of the shortage of brass, as one newly arrived "expert" in the antique business once volunteered. The fact is that handmade brass works clocks were far too expensive for the mass market. The incentive back of the effort to make reliable clocks with wooden gears was a purely commercial one. The all-metal clocks with their hand-filed gears, turned steel shafts, and elaborate brass dials, cost far too much for the average family.

Although Terry and a few others attempted to manufacture wooden works clocks it was not until about 1815 that Terry had begun to master the technique of not only making a serviceable wooden works clock but of making it cheaply enough to open up a vast market. None of these early wooden works clocks was laboriously cut out with the aid of a jackknife, as many people still think. Terry was by no means that crude. Rather they were gems of precision, considering their day. He had indeed contrived excellent machines not only for cutting his gear blanks from well-seasoned cherry wood but also for machine-cutting the gear teeth in them. He used water power to turn his lathes. He was the Henry Ford of the early clock business. Whereas the first few clocks (wooden works) made by Terry were peddled by him on horseback during the latter 1790's (none so far as the writers know are still in existence or recognized as such if they are); mass production came with the water power plant established by Terry at Plymouth, Connecticut, the power coming from a stream called Niagara Brook.

By 1820 Terry was doing a land-office business in wooden works clocks, having by that time introduced the now-famous and still-beautiful pillar and scroll case. Although this design has been attributed to him long since, recent research on the subject appears to give long-overdue credit for it to one Heman Clark, at one time an associate of Terry.

By far the larger number of early wooden works clocks were intended for shelf use, and not all clocks were sold complete with cases. Thousands were sold stripped and ready for casing. These were often cased by local cabinetmakers of the community, or purchasers sometimes made their own cases, usually of pine. Works intended both for tall cases and for shelf cases were often left caseless until the purchaser could get around to having a local joiner enclose the mechanism. This did not, however, prevent the use of the works in the meantime. When hung naked on the wall, such a

Fig. 86. (Left) The justly famous and scarce Eli Terry pillar and scroll wooden works clock with eighteenth century swan neck scroll, brass finials, slender pillars, and delicately scrolled bracket feet. *Circa* 1815. (Right) Later Federal-Empire pillar and scroll with heavy carving on mahogany. Choice clocks with wooden works are still not too difficult to find. Many thousands of such clocks were made during the 1820's and 1830's.

clock was called "wag-on-the-wall." The eight-day works permitted the weights (one for time, one for strike) to drop several feet; thirty hour works dropped only about twelve inches.

Later on, after Silas Hoadley, Riley Whiting, Chauncey Jerome, Seth Thomas, and others had set themselves up to profit in the market that Terry had opened, some attempt was made to develop an eight-day wooden works shelf clock. That some such clocks were marketed between 1825 and 1830 is known. Indeed, the writers have in their possession two beautifully cased wooden works shelf clocks, one by Terry and one by Thomas, intended for eight-day operation. Apparently, however, such clocks were never too successful and the fault was one of mechanism.

All of these clocks were operated by power generated by falling weights either of cast iron or, in the case of most cheap tall clocks, tin cylinders filled with stones or sand. Clearly the farther a weight of given poundage could fall, the longer a clock would run. Hence the so-called "tall clock." The only other way to obtain longer operation from a single winding was the use of heavier weights. The weights on the eight-day shelf clocks owned by the writers and mentioned above approximate eleven pounds each, while the weights in the more ordinary thirty-hour clocks with wooden works approximate two pounds. Naturally the eleven-pound weights of the eight-day clock took much longer to drop to the bottom of the clock case although they covered the same distance as the weights of the thirty-hour clocks.

The problem of the eight-day shelf clock was that of having wooden gear teeth hold up under the constant strain imposed on them by the heavy weights necessary to provide eight days of operation. As such gears got older they became less able to endure strain. Although some such clocks are still about, one should not cherish too much the idea of restoring them to usable condition. It can be done, but one might be awakened in the night by a released weight crashing through the bottom of a pet clock case.

If one wishes to have an operating thirty-hour wooden works clock, made during the 1820's or 1830's, there are still plenty of them about. At one time there were perhaps as many as one million such clocks in use. Unless the works have suffered unusual damage, they may be repaired at not too great a cost. Prices for such clocks may range all the way from $5 to $150, if one of the more desirable of the Terry or Thomas early pillar and scroll cases is involved. As a matter of fact, the price of such clocks is determined solely by the case, the condition, date, and design.

Within certain limits, there is a wide variety in case details between the years 1820 and 1835, although they all more or less follow the general type of the pillar and scroll. This is to be expected when it is recalled that many uncovered works were either peddled from house to house or sold to local jewellers who cased them. The general styles of the day were usually followed by those cabinet-makers who made cases. So far as the writers can determine, all of the larger clockworks producers of the time made their own clock cases or had a source for them. At the same time they also sold uncased works. Smaller producers were more inclined to make the whole clock, case included.

Oftentimes one will find the clock paper (old clocks are always more valuable, by the way, when the clock paper pasted back of the pendulum is intact) indicating both the name of the maker of the works and the name of the local jeweller who had it cased. The writers have in their collection a clock with a Riley Whiting works cased by one Wm. Whiting located on Chippewa Street in Buffalo, New York, during the early 1830's. Apparently some Connecticut clockmakers enjoyed a more brisk business in some particular part of the country than in others, a fact that appears to be borne out in the case of western New York where Riley Whiting wooden works are to be found in a ratio distinctly favorable to this theory. Out of twelve tall pine or grandfather cases locally made in western New York and discovered by the authors, eleven held Riley Whiting works. The twelfth was a Silas Hoadley wooden works.

Inasmuch as the cases of early wooden and brass works clocks in a large measure determine price, a few words on case style and evolution might be helpful.

Recent investigation appears to prove that Eli Terry must be taken down from the pedestal he has for so many years occupied as the originator of the charming pillar and scroll shelf clock case, a case so reminiscent of the late eighteenth century vogues with its brass finials and swan neck scroll. The pillars on either side of such clock cases were of small diameter and gracefully tapered. What is known of Terry's artistic nature also lends credence to the theory that the artistic skill demanded by the pillar and scroll case was beyond his talents. The man was obviously a mechanic although a very good one. It is now generally conceded that Heman Clark, one of Terry's contemporaries, was the designer of the case and that he in turn got his inspiration from some unknown, unsung fellow either in the later part of the eighteenth century or in the early part of the nineteenth. This pillar (especially) and scroll left its mark on clock case making history for many years, well into the 1860's or even later; and certainly long after thousands upon thousands of the lovely old wooden works clocks had passed on to their well-earned rest, either through storage in attics and barns or through cremation in the spring-cleaning trash pile.

The pillar and scroll enjoyed a brisk popularity for a few years in its purer form and it was produced by many imitators. Seth Thomas was among them. He was gentleman enough, however, to pay Terry for the right to manufacture the new and improved wooden works. Thomas also made many cases in the pillar and scroll manner. Indeed the cases made by the two men are practically identical, but the larger sums asked for such clocks favor Terry.

One would have to ask for a miracle if he wished to come upon one of the very rare Heman Clark pillar and scroll cases that were made a number of years before Terry's case appeared. The Heman Clark case held eight-day brass works, and was about one foot taller than either the Terry or Thomas later versions of it. Apparently Terry did not appear with a case of this type until about 1816.

Nor were Thomas, Terry, or Jerome the clock geniuses they later became in the public mind. Thomas and Terry were undoubtedly good mechanics with some flair for improvement, but authorities now agree that it was Joseph Ives and Heman Clark who rated as rare American inventors in the clock industry. Neither, it appears, possessed the business acumen of their more successful contemporaries. Jerome was something of a copyist; a very good exploiter of other people's good ideas.

It was not long after the successful introduction of the pillar and scroll case (it is known that not all early brass or wooden works shelf clocks made in the first twenty years of the nineteenth century were pillar and scroll; many were cased far more simply and are far more rare today) that certain modifications began to be made. For one thing the swan neck scroll at the top was changed to a more crudely scrolled single piece without benefit of finials, and the delicate pillars of the early Terry and Thomas cases were made heavier and placed on either side of the case in the form of pilasters, a concession to crudity made in the interests of cheaper produc-

FIG. 87. Simplified pilaster pillar and scroll, with stencils in place of carving, but still with wooden works. Such clocks were made well into the 1830's. Carved pineapple finials and claw feet.

tion. Thus a single turned pillar could be sawed in two lengthwise and the halves glued to either side of the clock case to reduce the expense.

It was also during the mid-1820's or even earlier that the case-makers took to using stencils both on the scrolled top piece or cornice and on the pilasters or columns, a practice that continued well into the 1840's. This permitted the use of pine and other wood in place of the more expensive mahogany. The sides of most clocks made during these times were covered with mahogany veneer. This was also used around the door frame. Some of the finest examples of the art of stencilling are still to be found on the pilasters and scrolled top board of clocks produced during these years.

Fig. 88. Showing the type of early stencilling used on the scrolled cornice of many clocks made between the 1820's and 1840's. An Ives pillar and scroll wooden work shelf clock produced during the early 1830's. A looking glass replaces the early painting.

More expensive clocks and clocks more in the spirit of Late American Empire appeared with carved mahogany pilasters, usually with various treatments of the then popular acanthus leaf motif. On such clocks it was also usual to carry the Empire decoration to the feet, which were carved in the form of claws. A further touch of 'Empire elegance was added by making the top board or cornice of thick mahogany and carving it to serve as a crest. The Terry company and others carved in eagles for the American trade and a crowned lion and shield for the Canadian trade. Like the stencilled clock, these strictly Empire affairs maintained their popularity well into the late 1830's.

Never before or since were such delightful scenes painted on glass as appeared on the clocks of the 1820's and 1830's. The early pillar and scrolls had village scenes, buildings of all sorts, including Mount Vernon and other bucolic views. These were framed with narrow bands of gold and black stencilling. Later, as the new versions of the pillar and scrolls grew in height and narrowed somewhat in width, the borders grew wider and perhaps less attractive, although the quality of both the painting and the stencilling was excellent. Occasionally one comes across old clocks showing the countenance of Washington and Jefferson, but most clocks bore scenes.

But let the reader not be too sure that every clock made between 1815 and 1835 meets the specifications outlined above or that the works are sure to be wooden. True, the great mass of clocks produced followed the popular trend. There were, however, many nonconformists; little fellows at work in the hinterlands who insisted on going their own way and who found customers who just wanted clocks without too much insistence upon the vogue. Either the prospect had to buy such a clock, or ride fifty or a hundred miles to get one more in vogue, or wait for the remote chance that a clock peddler might happen along.

The dials of these early clocks were almost without exception excellent examples of craftsmanship. They were invariably painted on a single piece of thin wood and supplied on the back with two cleats. Dials were usually painted white or buff with hand-painted numerals of delightful design; usually in Arabic, except in the case of banjos, and Roman numerals by a few of the above-mentioned nonconformists.

Speaking of banjos, it once more becomes necessary to lay an untruth or at least a popular misconception which insists upon giving the credit for the invention of this type of clock to Simon Willard. True, he did patent such a clock in this country but it was the works on which he made his improvements and not on the case design, which was introduced in England back in the 1770's.

The great era of the banjo lay between 1800 and 1835. The life of this popular clock did not end there but its artistic appeal and perfection ended thereabouts. The clock rode it out into the 1850's; but in forms that must have troubled not only the ghost of Simon Willard but also those of his two clockmaking brothers and the many other contemporaries, who, like those of Terry, copied Willard's patent without so much as a "thank you." Some were decent enough to leave their names off their clocks.

To the new collector who wishes a banjo, certain things should be said. First off, the price of the more desirable banjos not even bearing the name of any of the Willards begins at $300; and the price of the so-called "presentation Willard" signed by the master builder, Simon, is so high that the potential customer will have to choose between it and a new car.

If one should be offered an intact banjo in at least repairable condition for anything less than $150, he should be very suspicious unless the offer is made by a family or friend of long standing and the history of the clock is known.

Since more or less ordinary banjos sell at $300 to $500 each, they present a strong temptation to make reproductions with which to defraud gullible buyers. Excellent banjo works are being made in the United States today, exact copies of the Simon Willard works, and sold for about $35 each, a feat made easily possible with the aid of even modest machine shop equipment. Brass side-ornaments, exact copies of the old ones, are offered in several catalogues, as are the hand-painted glasses and the cast brass eagle finials. All an unscrupulous operator needs is the case, and that can be easily produced and readily made to appear to be old and reconditioned instead of being new.

The advisability of purchasing banjo clocks only from reliable people who will not fear to give a guarantee as to age, repairs, replacements, etc., is seen. It is no sin to make extensive repairs on old clocks. The sin consists in the dealer's not pointing them out.

Fig. 89. (1) Ogee clock with brass works, 1840's to 1880's. (2) Gothic clock, late 1840's to 1880's. (3) Late pillar clock 1850's to 1880's. (4) Modified Gothic, 1860's to 1880's. (5) Wall clock with spring, 1860's, 1870's. (6) Late Empire style 1850's, 1870's. (7) Late banjo, 1860's. (8) China clock, 1880's.

Many a badly mauled banjo has been seventy-five per cent restored and yet sold at a price for which a fairly good and true one could be had.

And now for the sadder story of the more truly Victorian shelf clocks, preparations for which were made in the early 1830's by Chauncey Jerome. For some time prior to this, American clock-makers either dreamed of a cheap all-brass clock works or tried their hands experimentally at making one from rolled brass sheet from England. The Connecticut metal people were trying to roll such brass in this country but were not making out at it. For one thing the inspiration of a prospective, truly large market for the product was lacking.

What Jerome dreamed of was a clock whose gear wheels could be punched out of relatively thin brass. Up to that time the clock-makers had either to cast blank wheels in brass themselves, or purchase them from suppliers. The gear teeth were laboriously filed out by hand with the aid of an indexing device or "engine," as it was then called. That meant a large number of man-hours for each clock works, so many that common folk could not afford to pay for them.

Apparently Chauncey Jerome did a heavy part of the dreaming about the great market for a cheap, high production clock with real brass works; while Heman Clark and Joseph Ives (especially the latter and a real genius he was!) did all of the inventing, credit for which, due to careless research, has for many years been given to Jerome. As Carl Dreppard, the authority, states in his recent excellent book devoted to clocks, Jerome had a positive genius for taking other people's ideas and getting credit for them. Ives not only experimented rather successfully with rolled brass gears but also made a number of successful works. Perhaps the only serious mistake he made was that of permitting Jerome to see them.

It should not be inferred that the brass works shelf clocks did not make their appearance until the 1830's. They were made for many years before that, but because of the tedious labor involved in their production they were too expensive to be popular. If rolled brass could be had, punches and dies could be made that would toss off gear wheels with a mere grunt. To Jerome must go the credit for the introduction of the cheap brass works and the stimulation thereby of the rolled brass industry, ever since a bulwark of Connecticut economy. Jerome was not long without competition in the field, being quickly followed by all of the larger producers who could afford the necessary tools and dies.

This development was swift but it did not, as many think, bring a sudden stop to the production of clocks with wooden works. There was an overlapping period of at least five years. One can still own a wooden works clock that is not as old as a clock with one of the earlier and cheaper brass works. This news will probably be most shocking to those who always felt that the wooden works goes back to the Year One.

All of the early clocks up to the 1860's, whether of brass or wood, were driven by falling weights which had periodically to be hoisted to the top of the case by means of a cord and a winding drum turned either by a key or a crank. This sort of power made for accuracy in timekeeping, the power supplied by the weight always being the same. This was unlike a coiled spring whose power output varied between the high tension immediately after winding and the low tension when winding was needed. For this reason, and due to expense and to its being more complicated, the spring was not used much in early clocks, if at all, by American clockmakers; although a spring-driven clock had been made and used by Henlein of Nuremberg before 1700. Weights were cheap and reliable and only their cords broke, whereas the breaking of a clock spring required a major operation.

Indeed it was not until the 1870's that the use of clock springs in the cheaper shelf clocks became widespread. That does not mean, however, that the weight suddenly passed out of existence at that time.

It was during the 1840's that clock case design and the execution of scenes and pictures began to suffer from the demands for still larger production. Especially did the faces of the clocks suffer. Dials made of sheet zinc became cruder and less artistic, the delicately stencilled border in gold was replaced, and the quaint little hand-painted scenes began to disappear. When they were used they were of a distinctly inferior quality. Soon the transfer (decalco- mania) was to come, and eliminate forever the charming panel art of earlier times.

FIG. 90. Maple Gothic, 1850's-1880's. Next to the ogee clock one of the most popular clocks made during Late Victorian times. Some are walnut, some maple, and some mahogany. Here the lower panel is of frosted glass.

Beginners in the collecting of antiques are likely to have a rather difficult time of it dating the various clocks made between 1845 and 1885. Even experts often scratch their heads. Although the clock business had by the 1860's settled down into the hands of a few very large producers, whose annual production was so great that 100,000 clocks of a single popular design was not unusual; each listed a larger number of different designs (involving the cases, mostly) and there was also considerable similarity between the products of the various companies. Some well-selling models were catalogued and sold for as many as twenty years. It is often difficult to distinguish between the clocks made in 1865 and those made in 1885. The tendency on the part of many antique dealers is to badly over-

FIG. 91. One of the several millions of the ogee clocks made during the Mid-Victorian and Late Victorian times. Occasionally such clocks are found with maple case (as shown) but still with the mahogany veneer on the ogee molded front. Often they showed state capitol buildings on the lower glass. This one illustrates the capitol at Albany, N. Y. The picture was produced by transfer.

estimate the age of the clocks made during the 1860-1885 period. Not only that, but they also badly overrate the scarcity of such things. Millions of clocks were produced between the years mentioned and most middle- and upper-class American homes were able to boast of having anywhere from two to ten clocks, depending upon the size of the house and family.

The clocks of the years after the 1840's were indeed the real achievement of mass production in this country as it related to metal products. Like the works, the cases were turned out by the hundreds of thousands. On the whole, the choice of the present purchaser must rest on the case rather than on the works built between the 1840's and the 1880's. The works up to the introduction of the spring-driven clock were practically all the same, and therefore there was very little to recommend one clock works over another.

FIG. 92. Late china clock (probably 1890's) but in keeping with such clocks made during the 1880's. Finer types are hand painted.

A few of the cases introduced during the latter part of the 1840's remained popular for many years. It was during this time that the so-called "steeple" clock or, more properly, the Gothic clock, was introduced. This turned out to be a winner, holding its ground for many years, and the ladies still go for it, which is proven by the fact that such clocks usually sell for twice as much as other clocks from the same period. There is little or nothing on these clocks that will permit the amateur collector quickly to supply it with a birthday.

The so-called acorn clock was also brought out in the late 1840's but never became quite as popular as the Gothic design. It sold for at least twenty-five years, however.

The winner over them all in public acceptance and the clock most in evidence today was the so-called "ogee" thirty-hour clock, made both in large and in medium size and first introduced some-

FIG. 93. One of the more beautiful of the fine glass case French clocks of the Late Victorian period. Decorated with rhinestones and blue cloisonne. (Courtesy Olde Lamps, Inc., Buffalo, N. Y.)

time during the 1840's. The larger ones were about eighteen inches tall, sixteen inches wide and four and a half inches thick. The larger size were most popular. These were two-weight, brass works affairs with a time train and a striking train. It was about this time that the coiled spring gong was introduced which provided a deep, resonant tone instead of the thin tinkle of the old cast-iron bells.

All these clocks were provided with a door divided just above center with a veneered cross member which marked off the face opening. Below these appeared a transfer picture, floral decoration, or some other sort of ornamentation of that kind. A few of the early ogee clocks had hand-painted pictures instead of transfers, but these clocks are now hard to find. The paintings were distinctly inferior to those done during the 1820's and 1830's.

Tall clocks of a sort were still being made in the 1840's, and perhaps here and there a fellow of the old school was to be found who would do a creditable job. By and large, however, the tall clocks made during these days were not too good nor were they then too popular. They passed out of favor almost entirely after 1850.

Among the clock oddities of the 1870's were the cases cast in iron, in the form of Topsy, Little Sambo, etc. They were called blinking eye clocks, the clock mechanism causing a painted piece of metal back of the eye openings in the cast iron to shift from side to side.

During the 1870's also, the so-called cast bronze clock made a bid for popularity, but if one is to judge by the frequency with which the survivors are now found in the antique shops, such clocks did not enjoy wide distribution. The cases were of cast metal and were highly ornamental, having romantic figures, horses, cherubs, etc. Some were cast in iron and finished in bronze, and the better ones were cast in pure bronze.

It is also to be noted that a few clock cases of smaller size appeared in papier-mâché during the late 1840's and early 1850's. These were hand painted and boasted mother-of-pearl inlay. They are very scarce today. Most of them were imported from France.

CHAPTER IX

Mirrors

DURING early Victorian times the coquettes and the Beau Brummells had just as much desire to inspect their toilettes with a mirror as do the modern fops and man-hunters, both genteel and uninhibited. Hence the tremendous number of mirrors produced between 1825 and 1860. Some homes boasted half a dozen or more. And why not? Even as early as the 1820's one could purchase a presentable mirror for as little as one or two dollars; these mirrors would sell today for twenty times their original cost.

There is still to be found a mirror or looking glass for every need of the collector devoted to the furnishings of the Victorians, and most such mirrors are in good or fair taste, especially the earlier ones. They may be had for the dressing table, the bureau, the mantel, or the hall.

The most charming mirrors of the nineteenth century, however, appeared before Victorian times. Those in vogue between the years 1820 and 1840 are especially delightful. Many of these had a small horizontal divider across the top of the mirror setting off a rectangle of glass, upon the back of which appeared a quaint pastoral scene or one showing ships or buildings of some sort. Some were without dividers or painted scenes. These were usually intended for more opulent homes and were more intricate in design. Most such mirror frames were in mahogany and only rarely does one come across them done in maple, although these are to be had.

The design of these earlier mirrors followed a rather definite pattern, a carry-over from the latter part of the eighteenth century in so far as the top cornice was concerned. This cornice overhung the top of the mirror by an inch or so, with or without a recess in the center. The underside of the cornice was decorated with turned wooden balls or acorns of small size. The columns on either side of such mirrors were often of the so-called rope or spiral turning pattern. When not so done, the columns often had a more classical form in true Empire style.

Fig. 94. Provincial mirrors of the 1820's. Sausage-shaped pilasters covered with gesso and painted black. Brass rosettes in corners of pine frame.

Many of these mirrors were also produced with formal gilt finish. It is rare to find such a mirror today with the gilt finish in a state of good preservation, and when so found the price asked may be high.

On the whole, the mirrors produced before the 1820's were more delicate and in better taste than those that appeared after the Americans began what might be called the "ponderous era" of Empire furniture, when apparently the components of all furniture had to be twice as heavy as needed.

It was during this time that the first-mentioned mirrors were made. Some of the latter styles still carried the cornice with the down-hanging balls and acorns, but the simpler forms did not have this ornamentation. They had sausage-shaped pilasters around the whole of the frame, with a little brass rosette arranged in each corner. The picture panel at the top was usually included, was always well done and quaint, and very much in the manner of the pictures on the contemporary clock doors. When such a mirror is found with the divider intact but with a small mirror above it in place of the picture that once occupied their spot, this may be taken as evidence that the dealer has not bothered to have a new picture painted and inserted. Not many of these quaint little pictures have come down to us in good shape. Such replacement paintings today usually cost about ten dollars when done by people who have the special talent needed for painting backwards on glass surfaces.

The better-class mirror of this type is done in gold leaf, which finish has usually failed to take the abuse of a hundred and twenty years with much grace. If the mirror is so worn as to be unpresentable, the purchaser should take with a grain of salt any statement that regilding with gold leaf may be done for a few dollars, even if there may be a place near home to have such work done. Even the best of the gold bronze paints applied with a brush are none too good.

Also among mirrors of this type made during the late Empire period are those with carved pilasters or with columns having acanthus leaf decoration. These are on the rare side, however, and smart dealers usually place a rather stiff price tag on them, the larger types being likely to bring up to one hundred dollars.

Most if not all of the (then) cheaper mirrors of this sort were painted black or deep brown with touches of gilt between the sausage turnings. Here refinishing is not much of a chore, and a touch of bronze gilt may pass without drawing too much notice.

These mirrors continued to be the vogue for some twenty years, finally becoming passé in the late 1830's when they began to be replaced by the so-called ogee mirror. This in turn held sway for many years, carrying well into the 1860's. It was a simple pine frame, wide, covered with good mahogany veneer, and plain, with no ornamentation whatsoever. How this mirror was able to survive in its original and somewhat naked form throughout a period that as a whole was so debased by excessive ornamentation is a first rate

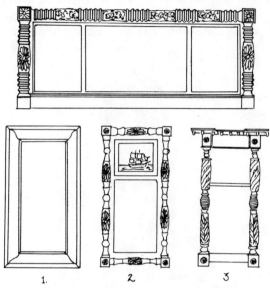

1.   2.   3.

Fig. 95. (Top) A massive mantel mirror of the Late Empire period, probably made sometime in the 1830's. The frames of such mirrors were invariably covered with gold leaf. (1) So-called ogee mirror. Early ones (1830's) were narrower, and those with crotch mahogany veneer usually had gold leaf molding on inner and outer edges. A few such mirrors to be found in curly maple. This general type of mirror was popular into the 1860's. Made in large and small sizes. (2 and 3) Mirrors of the Late American Empire period. *Circa* 1825.

mystery. However, thousands of such mirrors did finally suffer the humiliation of a dose of white paint. But let no collector unafraid of paint remover or soiled hands pass up such maltreated articles when bids are asked at country auctions. Even the small mirror of this type now commands a price of from twelve to fifteen dollars, while the larger ones suitable for mantel use bring from thirty to forty dollars.

The earliest of the so-called ogee mirrors are easily distinguished from the later types with the crotch mahogany veneered frames. The early ones also had crotch mahogany veneering but each frame had gilt molding around the outside and around the mirror. A few such mirrors are still about, but they are difficult to find.

Fig. 96. One of the finer types of mahogany dresser mirrors of the Early Victorian period. Piecrust molding around the skirt. Later dresser mirrors were more apt to be without lower compartment and drawers.

The period between 1825 and 1840 also brought forth another type of Empire mirror. This was called a cheval glass and was a mirror mounted in a floor stand and arranged on a swivel. A full-length body view was possible with such mirrors when the viewer stood back a few feet.

On the whole the framework of these mirrors was massive, and the pillars holding the mirror were of mahogany or cherry and heavily carved with either spirals or the acanthus leaf.

The so-called dressing mirror of Victorian times was more apt to be without a drawer. It will be recalled that such mirrors were made for mounting on chests. Practically all of them made before Victorian times had either one, two, or three small drawers in a case upon which the mirror standards were fixed. This does not mean to say that all Victorian dressing mirrors were without drawers, but it is safe to assume that most of them were. Many of those appearing between 1845 and 1865 had heavily scrolled frames, brackets, and baseboard, all of them covered with crotch mahogany veneer.

Those among the early Victorians who did not use such dressing mirrors, hung the more sedate ogee mirrors back of their dressing tables or chests of drawers. These mirrors are still to be found in large numbers, a fact that vouches for their once great and deserved popularity.

The eighteenth century cult to the contrary notwithstanding, these mirrors had a simple dignity about them. Certainly they were to be preferred to the disastrously ornate Chippendale and Hepplewhite mirrors of the 1780–90 era. The tops of many of these mirrors, with their gilded cords, Grecian urn finials, and dangling whatnots, look as though they had been targets of an assortment of Christmas tree ornaments, many of which stuck.

One occasionally comes across early mirrors of the ogee type done in figured maple, although they are difficult to discover. They are usually the product of individual craftsmen and much to be desired. One may without too much trouble and expense assemble a maple chair, chest, bed, and bedside stand, but the maple mirror may take months or even years of search unless one is lucky.

Pine frame mirrors are easily achieved by the purchase of an ogee mirror with mahogany veneer beyond repair. This veneer was always placed on soft pine frames because of good adhesion for the glue. If the veneering is completely removed, an excellent pine mirror frame will be left.

CHAPTER X

Victorian Pictures

NO ROOM whether parlor, dining room, or bedroom can be authentically Victorian without a picture or two: lithograph, engraving, or painting. The Victorians were the first of the Americans who could afford plentifully to decorate their walls with works of art or what they thought to be works of art. The ability to do this did not result from the growing wealth of the country so much as it resulted from the perfection in this country of the German-invented process of lithography, a development that eventuated finally in the establishment of a number of American lithography houses, among them the Kellogg Brothers of Hartford, Connecticut, and, of more lasting fame, N. Currier, and (later) Currier and Ives of New York City.

Come the 1840's, the works of the American lithographers became so generally available to housewives and at such reasonable prices that few homes went without a few dashes of color on the walls. Small uncolored prints could be had for a few cents, larger ones in color for a few dollars. During the 1860's, for instance, Currier and Ives were advertising their now-rare scenes, colored and in large folio (26 by 36 inches), for three dollars each.

The person interested in the creation of an authentic Victorian room is not necessarily interested in scarce Currier and Ives prints or any other lithographic rarity. He is interested primarily in creating the atmosphere he seeks with a minimum of expense. Fortunately the remaining mass of Currier and Ives pictures still on sale in the shops makes the problem a very simple one. Millions of Currier and Ives prints were sold during the fifty-odd years the company was in existence. Today many of these prints are available for anywhere from a dollar to five dollars. Much depends upon the subject, the size (folio) of the print, whether it is colored or black and white, and its general condition as regards fox marks, water stains, and, above all, its margins. Of course, if one is interested simply in hanging a few Currier and Ives to achieve a Victorian effect, the matter of margin is not important. However, should one wish to hang some of the more important and therefore more expensive of the Currier and Ives prints for which one may have to pay from twenty-five to fifty dollars, one should not permit the dealer to tell him that a cropped margin does not detract from the value of such things. Many collectors of Currier and Ives will have nothing to do with prints having cropped margins, and cropping was common practice in the days before people could run out to a chain store for a frame of the proper size.

The beginner must also watch for Currier and Ives reproductions that have been treated with chemicals to give them the brownish appearance of age. When anything over five dollars is to be paid, one wishes to be sure not only that the dealer from whom the picture is purchased is scrupulous but also that he knows enough about such prints not to have been victimized himself, in the first place. Above all, the beginner should shy away from Currier rarities offered at bargain prices. The big city markets for them is still brisk enough to absorb them at high prices.

When it is known that Currier and Ives alone, to say nothing of the other lithographers, produced over five thousand picture titles, it will be seen that any listing or anything beyond generalized instructions for buying would be impossible here.

Among the poorest-selling of the Currier and Ives lithos, either early or late, are the baby-faced little girls and boys, once so extremely popular. They must have been popular because they have been handed down from year to year by the thousands. Such prints alone (they were usually colored) are never worth more than a dollar or so. Yet these things are as Victorian as the Queen's bustle. The temperance pictures and the pictures having to do with moral subjects in general are still to be had, on the whole, at low prices.

Listed below, the reader will find the subjects once offered by Currier and Ives that now demand the highest prices. However, no effort has been made at price classification. All are good Americana.

1. Sporting scenes of hunting, boxing, horse racing, etc.

2. Railroad scenes of all kinds, all of them showing the old wood-burning locomotives

3. Sailing ships, racing yachts, clippers, etc.

4. Fire scenes, firemen in action, engines, etc.

5. Country scenes and country homes, both in winter and summer

6. Flower and fruit prints suitable for dining room use. These are not rare, but good examples bring twenty-five dollars because of demand.

The lithographers did not supply the only pictures needed for the authentic reproduction of Victorian rooms. Many other types of art available for hanging can be found and at very low cost. There are still to be found many fine engravings both small and large, paintings in oil and water colors, drawings, etc.

The *Peterson Magazine* and Godey's *Lady's Book* of the 1840's and 1850's are rich sources both of very romantic steel engravings and of the style pictures wherein the ladies appear in the latest fashions and each print is hand colored. These books have come down from Victorian attics in large numbers, so large indeed that whole bound volumes containing a number of the style pictures and engravings may still be had for three or four dollars or even less, making the pictures cost little more than twenty-five cents each. The quaint engravings, many of which reveal the yearnings of young female hearts, can be made especially attractive by the addition of color. This can be applied by print dealers for as little as one dollar or less.

Among the larger steel engravings current and popular during the 1860's are those of the famed Sartain who did both the Washington and Lincoln families, among other suitable subjects. One may still find such engravings suitably framed for as little as five dollars, often less, especially in the secondhand stores. Lincoln shown with Mary and their sons in the drawing room of the White House was an especially popular piece in the North although a reward might safely be offered for the discovery of such a thing in the South.

Both the Lincolns and the Washingtons are also available in oval engravings made to fit the very popular (then and now!) walnut oval frames of the 1850's and 1860's. So many were the subjects offered in the form of steel engravings during the 1860's and 1870's that the collector is bound to find something that will satisfy him, and that at a very low price.

Fig. 97. A typical Early or Mid-Victorian oil painting of the romantic school with plain molded gilt frame.

During early and mid-Victorian times, young ladies from well situated middle-class families attended academies where, among other things, they were given instruction in oil painting. Countless thousands of oil paintings were made by these students upon returning home. Some were good, some were bad artistically speaking, but all of them make good Victorian art today. With a little shopping it is not difficult to find such paintings in excellent gilt frames for a few dollars. The dates may range from the 1830's to the 1890's.

Over the last few years family portraiture in oil from early or mid-Victorian times have become very popular especially in pairs showing man and wife, brother and sister, etc. This was indeed the golden age of family portraiture in oil, no family worthy of social notice neglecting to arrange portraits for posterity by way of a professional job in oil. Not a few such paintings were done with skill, the prices asked by the big city artists amounting to several hundred dollars. A hundred dollars was not an uncommon price to pay for such work even in the smaller communities. Then there was the itinerant limner, the unschooled fellow who went about the

Fig. 98. A fine example of one of the better types of oval portrait frames used during the 1840's and 1850's.

countryside painting people in the rural districts on a sort of catch-as-catch-can basis.

Portraits painted by the itinerant limners who worked during the first half of the nineteenth century are now rated among our most valuable and interesting Americana from that era. True, they were stiff, crude, and painted from a primary palette that offered no subtlety of color, yet these old portraits possess a great deal of charm.

The same is true concerning the scenic primitives painted or drawn between 1830 and 1880. The untrained purchaser of such works should not be too sure that he recognizes the requisites of a good primitive without first consulting either Carl Drepperd's *American Pioneer Arts and Artists* or *American Primitive Painting* by Jean Lipman. An inexperienced collector may pay a high price for what he believes to be a good specimen of primitive painting or folk art only to discover later that it was copied from an early instruction book or a popular picture of the day. The good primitive came from the utterly untutored artist and individualist who had

Fig. 99. A Mid-Victorian shadow box with cast wax scene and figures illustrating one of the Christian Crusades.

his own way of doing things, crude though they were. He knew nothing about form, technique, color, perspective, or any of the remaining qualifications needed by orthodox artists. Good primitives appear not only in oil but also in water color, tempera, pencil, and pen.

No treatment of the subject of Victorian art would be complete without mention of that often too-ugly-for-words thing they call the shadow box. It was a frame behind which was a deep box lined with silk, satin, or other material and in which all manner of things were placed in what passed for artistic arrangement. Some contained homemade displays, some were purchased already supplied with wax fruit or flowers or other items. Some of the larger boxes were two feet wide, some of the smaller ones only a few inches and oval in form. One of the most treasured shadow boxes in the possession of the writers takes the form of half the size of an oval walnut frame and displays delicately arranged waxed flowers.

Some shadow boxes were oblong, some were hexagonal (very ugly), some were round, and some were oval. Few were artistic.

FIG. 100. The better type of gilt oblong frame used between the late 1820's and 1850's. This one covers a shadow box with a Parian head.

Occasionally one finds a shadow box with a homemade display presenting braided samples of the hair of the living and deceased members of a family, done in wreaths and set among other items representing the artistic taste of the person who arranged the melancholy layout, probably some time in the 1860's or 1870's. No doubt such morbid forms of art could be attributed to the emotional disturbance occasioned by the Civil War.

Rarer by far among the shadow boxes are the small scenes done in cast wax, usually with religious motifs. One of them involves an assemblage that initiated one of the crusades, obviously Catholic in significance. Still more rare are the shadow boxes with heavy gilt (and very good, too!) oblong frames having oval openings. An oblong box lined with black velvet was placed back of the oval opening and had mounted in it a Parian head of a woman very "Greekish" and classical in tone.

The reader may not wholly relish the shadow box in any form, awkward as they appear on walls and more often than not of highly questionable artistic value. Yet for the person who assembles an authentic Victorian atmosphere of the 1850's or 1860's. the shadow box should be considered almost a "must." What is more, it is the feeling of these writers, their amateur status fully considered and their opinion given with full humility, that as the years go on and the Victorian period gains more solid possession of its claim to antiquity, such things will be eagerly sought and handsomely paid for. After all, the spurned art of one day becomes eventually the prized items of another day, all accomplished by the strange magic of the passing years. Attics are like wine cellars where things mellow and grow old and more valuable. Finally, the trash of yesteryear emerges into the light of a new day with reborn appreciation, and no one can account fully for the strange magic wrought during the attic interlude and the rebirth of interest. Such are the strange workings of the human mind.

If the reader wants to avoid the inclusion of the daguerreotype in his or her Victorian parlor, a reconsideration is advised. Two or three of these, even if one cannot boast of the subjects as relatives, add a little necessary touch to the desired total effect. Many of the most expensive cases containing these "tintypes" are nothing less than charming, let the scoffers say what they will. The tintypes along with the ambrotype (later) persisted from the 1840's to the 1880's, finally being swept out of existence by the inventions of one George Eastman.

If this precariously poised civilization of ours does not collapse altogether, daguerreotypes now offered for a dollar or so will some day command twenty times that price. There will come a time when "ancestor" pictures on tinplate will be in as much demand as the "ancestor" oil paintings done a hundred years ago, which now command as much as one hundred dollars for an acceptable pair, say a man and wife of the 1840's.

Still to be sought and found among the rapidly disappearing examples of Early and Mid-Victorian folk art are the little framed flower pictures done with colored tin foil and set back of openings in an otherwise black piece of glass. Most of them are crude and childish, but if the reader is young let him or her watch the quoted prices of such articles over the years ahead. We are now in that transition period of Victorian appreciation when we, like the early mid-Victorians, are caught laughing at the furniture of our more immediate forefathers. The Victorian did not really stop laughing until after the Queen died in 1901, but a hint of what was to come was noticeable at the Philadelphia Centennial in 1876 where a display of colonial furniture was featured. This Exhibition celebrated the one hundredth anniversary of the opening of the Revolutionary war. Apparently the passing of one hundred years does something peculiar to the human mind, quickens its appreciation for the dignity of age, for the graces and charms of bygone days. Although one hundred years has been set quite arbitrarily as the minimum age of anything to be dignified by the term antique, that length of time nevertheless seems curiously well suited to purely human feeling in such matters.

One of the most charming and sedate among all of the possible wall decorations of Victorian times is the silhouette. Many and beautiful were these dainty cuttings produced during the first half of the nineteenth century, the more nearly perfect of the existing specimens displaying an almost unbelievable delicacy. Some involved portraiture, either head, bust, or full figure; some scenes, some flowers, and some animals. Some were mounted in small square frames, some in small walnut oval frames. In any form and with any subject, these things are among the most acceptable of the art objects bequeathed to us by the Victorians. However, they are not cheap unless one happens upon a new arrival among the dealers who has not yet learned too much about what is good or what is not so good. Especially desirable are the full figures showing little girls with their pantalets, ladies with their hoopskirts, or gentlemen in their cutaways and beaver hats.

So closely are picture frames associated with suitable art that a helpful word about them may not be amiss. There are still large numbers of the 1860–85 type of plain walnut and black gesso frames to be found, although the prices of the solid walnut variety have gone suddenly upward in the past few years. Time was (and not too far back) when one could have all one could carry home for as little as fifty cents each. Nowadays they bring from three to ten dollars each, depending upon size, condition, and the part of the country where they are offered for sale.

Due to the present scarcity of the oval walnut frames, the deep oblong walnut frame with gold bands has come forward to take its place and prices asked for these have reacted accordingly. Unlike many of the better types of picture frames used during the Early and Mid-Victorian periods, these later walnut varieties were able to take much more abuse. On the other hand many of the Early Victorian frames were of pine, covered with either plain molded gesso or figured gesso. Both had gold-leaf finish. This gesso, a sort of plaster-of-Paris, was extremely brittle; and few such frames, either plain or figured, have survived without being chipped or having been covered with cheap bronze paint.

Not a few of the larger portrait frames of the 1840's and 1850's were of the oval and ornamental type and these are today relatively scarce. The writers have rarely seen them offered for less than twenty-five dollars each and this minus the portrait. Oval in shape, too, were the openings in many of the larger oblong gilt frames popular in the 1820's and to the 1840's. These may run as high as fifty dollars each, depending upon condition.

One may spend hundreds or even thousands of dollars in purchasing Victorian art. One the other hand a budget of twenty-five dollars or even less, carefully spent, may supply half a dozen rooms with suitable pictures in oil, pen, pencil, or lithography. That may require quite a bit of shopping about, even in the secondhand stores. But isn't that part of the fun?

And then there is the glass dome with its wax flowers, or fruit, or draped crosses, always a safe and sure thing to use in establishing a Victorian atmosphere. Fortunately, not all glass domes merit the abuse that has been heaped upon domes in general. Occasionally one

Fig. 101. One of the more acceptable glass domes covering a display of wax flowers with a real monarch butterfly. Many glass dome displays were homemade.

comes upon a smaller and more artistically executed work under a dome that is perhaps no more than ten inches high. The contents of the glass domes, too, may be worth-while Americana, namely the handiwork of the artistic and near-artistic young ladies who carefully shaped sheets of tinted wax into all manner of flora and fauna. Such work was among the evening pastimes of the 1860's and 1870's.

In those days young ladies could purchase the little hand tools (fifteen in number); the wax molds for pears, bananas, peaches, and apples; and Madam Scheifflele's imported tinted wax sheets at any art store. On sale, too, were accessories; among them wire, powdered colors, stamens, arrowroot, sprig moss, frosting, spirit lamps, and leaf molds.

Good judgment in selecting an example or two of such work will not only help to preserve an almost-lost home craft, but the small investment will also be a sound one. The day of the glass dome has yet to arrive. The not-too-distant future will make present prices appear very low indeed.

CHAPTER XI

China

THE complete story of pottery and china is an involved one, the telling of which would require several volumes the size of the present work. Because of limited space, only an over-all outline can be given here. An attempt will be made to familiarize the reader with a little of the terminology of the china collector and some of the types of collectible china found in the average antique shop.

When the authors began frequenting the better antique shops some years ago, they were floored when terms like "hard paste," "Belleek," "porcelain," "crossed swords," "Parian," etc., were used. Diligently they searched for some sort of single book giving definitions of such terms. None, apparently, was available and the following explanations will in some measure at least attempt to fill this need.

An expert will say very quickly that the paste used in making china is coarse and thick or creamy white or that the paste has bluish or greenish tints. He can also tell whether the glaze is creamy white or glossy or thickly spread so that it collects in "tears"—all by simply holding a piece to the light and feeling it. It is not the purpose of this book to develop an expert, however. Many years of study and experience would be necessary before one could hope instantly to check the grade of china by surface appearance and feel.

The beginner can best learn from actual instruction from a person who knows china. To have the fine points of a Dresden piece pointed out while holding that piece is far more valuable than reading about it or studying a picture of it.

Most collectors like nothing better than to show and explain the fine points of their treasures to an interested neophyte. The authors' advice, therefore, is for the beginner to build up a knowledge of the fundamentals first, then find a person who knows and learn from experience.

China collecting need not be an expensive hobby. True, if one collects only the Meissen "Onion" pattern, for example, each piece represents considerable outlay. As an instance, the authors recently saw a large tureen in that pattern selling for $450. Such prices being

FIG. 102. Blue pattern Ironstone platter of the 1870's.

out of the question and liking the deep blue pattern, they collect Onion made by English firms at later dates. No matter what the budget or tastes, china collecting on a modest scale is possible.

The terminology in china collecting is somewhat confusing to the beginner but is really very simple. There are three main divisions: pottery, semichina, and china which is really porcelain. All have the same basic ingredient: clay. Pottery and semichina are made from clay with impurities. China, or porcelain, is made of clay which is purified and refined before baking.

Porcelain, which comes from the Italian word *porcellana* (meaning cowry) was imported from China by the Portuguese and Dutch in the seventeenth century. The Chinese made their products from a special clay called kaolin. Because of the superiority of the ware from China over the pottery being made in Europe, it became popular and English potters, after experimenting, began to make porcelain, or china, as it was called.

The terms china and porcelain are really synonymous according to the dictionary which defines china as porcelain or porcelainware

FIG. 103. Three pieces of a choice pink luster teaset. *Circa* 1860's. (Courtesy Mrs. Penn Perkins, Lockport, N. Y.)

and porcelain as china or chinaware. The words are used interchangeably.

Through the use of various clays and the addition of other substances, many types of chinaware or porcelain have been developed.

The various terms may be defined as follows:

PORCELAIN. Translucent ware, usually white and glazed.

PASTE. The substance of which the body of an article of china or porcelain is made.

HARD PASTE. Fine-grained and glossy, made from natural clay. Often called "true porcelain."

Soft Paste. Dull, porous, and made of artificial clay; often called "natural porcelain."

Glaze. The shiny material covering the paste.

Hard Glaze. Thin and without color.

Soft Glaze. Can be scratched and is somewhat gummy.

Faience. A French word applied to all glazed earthenware.

Majolica. A type of faience; all glazed earthenware, originally Italian decorated pottery of the fifteenth, sixteenth, seventeenth, and eighteenth centuries.

Biscuit. Pottery or porcelain before being enamelled or glazed.

Pottery. Wares which are entirely opaque and not translucent, generally formed of colored clay.

Earthenware. Broad term covering all pieces made of clay and baked.

Stoneware. Ware in which the glazing and firing are done at one time, usually accomplished by introducing salt in the kiln.

Semichina. Made with a large admixture of feldspar.

The reader will find, however, that a factory making china or porcelain, bisque or earthenware is called a pottery; and a man who manufactures any ware made of clay, a potter. The term pottery when broadly used includes any article made from clay.

Any attempt to include a description of all the types of china, pottery, and stoneware would be futile. There are many excellent books covering each of the fields. The following pages will merely try to highlight a few of the types available. Most of these are being treated because they are the most collectible and most often found in the shops.

Meissen (Dresden)

Although real Meissen or Dresden, as it is usually called, is far beyond the financial reach of the Victorian collector and chronologically out of line, the term is so often used that a short explanation seems to be in order. The story is a fascinating one.

John Frederick Böttcher (Johann Friedrich Böttger) was an

apothecary's apprentice in Berlin. His experiments in connection with his search for the philosophers' stone became known to both the King of Prussia and the King of Saxony. When he fled to Saxony the Prussian King had him brought back under guard and set him up in a laboratory in Meissen, near Dresden. All this happened in 1705. In his laboratory he developed true or hard-paste porcelain.

Fig. 104. More common type bisque figurines popular during the 1880's. Courtesy Mrs. Penn Perkins.

After his death, the figures which we associate with the name of Meissen or Dresden were made at Meissen. The Dresden shepherdess with her looped-up skirt, her laced bodice, tiny slippers, and large hat was originated in Meissen; as well as the pattern for the figurines, groups showing ladies in coaches, ladies doing any number of things, but all dainty, colorful, and fragile.

This type of figure has been in the process of duplication all through the years and, indeed, still is. Another pattern originated by Meissen and copied through the years is the famous Onion pattern. The "onion" is really a Chinese peach or pomegranate. Many are the collectors of Onion, whether it be Meissen, English, or Dutch Onion; it is one of the collectible patterns difficult to find in quantity and fairly expensive because of its unavailability.

Now a word about the crossed swords marking. It is an underglaze blue marking first used in Meissen in 1725. However, it must be pointed out that crossed swords on the bottom of a piece do not necessarily indicate age. This mark has been used on adaptations and is still so used. Checking with a book that gives markings vs. years should certainly be resorted to if any great outlay of money is involved.

Bisque

Bisque is unglazed, pure white porcelain with a matlike finish. It was made in Sevres, as early as 1750. Most collectors' interest, however, lies in the bisque made in the nineteenth century, much of it in the latter part.

The bulk of bisque articles is in the form of statuettes or figurines and decorated in soft blues, pinks and greens with occasional touches of gold. They were generally made in pairs: a boy and a girl, two girls, etc. Usually when one is found alone, it means that the mate has been broken.

Match holders, toothpick holders, doll heads, etc., were also made in bisque. Some have hollow bases, some are solid. Of course the quality of these figurines differs from fine to relatively undesirable. At any rate, ordinary collectors with ordinary amounts of money to spend can still have a lot of fun putting together a small bisque collection.

Parian

Parian is a distinct form of porcelain which is so named because of its resemblance to the white marble once quarried on the island of Paros in the Aegean Sea. This marble was used by sculptors, and the Parian porcelain which was developed to make miniature busts and statues was first called statuary ware.

Parian was developed in England in the middle 1880's and because of demand was made in great quantities. For example, one English concern made more than 450,000 pieces annually. Much of this Parian ware was shipped to the United States, which accounts for its relative abundance in our shops today. It was made in all manner of forms: pitchers, vases, busts, candlesticks, doll heads, and trinket boxes, to mention but a few.

A coarse white biscuit and Parian-like porcelain was once made at Bennington, Vermont. This is not, of course, true Parian. Probably much of what is found and collected is not true Parian and should be called Parian-type or biscuit porcelain.

A simplified explanation (possibly too simplified to suit the expert) is that true Parian is a porcelain which is poured into the molds while hot, instead of being molded into shape. There is a type of ware which resembles Parian and is called Parian by some. It comes in blue, yellow, brown, and green backgrounds with white raised designs. Of these the blue is most often found. Most authorities agree, however, that Parian is white and white only.

Belleek

This is a development of Parian and should be discussed in connection with it. Belleek is biscuit porcelain with a glaze of unusual luster. Made in Ireland and known as Irish Belleek, dinnerware of this sort has become well known to lovers of fine china. What is not so well known is that the best Belleek was made in the United States between 1870 and 1890. It was made in large quantities; consequently most collectible Belleek is probably of American manufacture.

Staffordshire

How many of the smaller antique dealers do love to mouth this much-abused word! To many, Staffordshire means the old deep blue scenic plates, platters, pitchers, etc. The term, however, covers much territory; for the Staffordshire district, known in England as The Potteries, is where Spode, Wedgwood, Minton, Turner, Wood, and others had their manufactories.

Thus the term is too inclusive. Many types of ware came from many potteries bearing the name Staffordshire and often in small letters the initials or name of the potter. It seems to the authors that this was one of the first institutional trade-marks; one of the first instances of the banding together of a group of artisan producers to establish a name for a good product.

The word Staffordshire on a plate is good, but it shouldn't double the price!

Wedgwood

No discussion of china is complete without the inclusion of Wedgwood, still being made today and cherished as fine china. It had its beginning in England in the 1700's.

Josiah Wedgwood, the pioneer, was born in 1730, the son of a man who worked as a potter in his youth. As an aftermath of smallpox, young Wedgwood spent a large part of his youth as an invalid. He became a dreamer and his dreams turned to the problem of designing and making the most beautiful pottery in the world.

By the time he was thirty, this dreamer had his own pottery and quickly became a world-famous maker of pottery. He was appointed potter to Her Majesty Queen Charlotte and at thirty-nine was commissioned to make a dinner set for the Empress of Russia. These honors were due to his artistry and his mania for perfection. Daily, Wedgwood walked through his plant brushing from the benches with his cane those pieces he thought to be unworthy of his name.

There are two main types of Wedgwood: the ornamental and the useful. Jasperware, probably the one which most people associate with the name of Wedgwood, was pottery with a dark background of blue, lilac, green, or yellow, having white, cameo-like decoration. The other, queensware, named for Queen Charlotte, was a cream-colored, fine-textured china made by Wedgwood for table use.

Although jasperware pitchers, teasets, etc., signify Wedgwood to the neophyte, the output of his potteries included lamps, medallions, cameos for jewelry, trinket holders, busts for tombs, chessmen, and cribbage boards, to mention but a few.

Spode

Here is another name synonomous with fine china. Founded by Josiah Spode (the first of three Josiahs) in 1776, this pottery introduced the blue underglaze printing which made Staffordshire so famous. He also became noted for his Chinese designs (for example, Willow), for his Egyptian red teapots and jugs, and for some pieces usually associated with Wedgwood. Famous Spode patterns include Willow, Peacock, Italian (a view of Roman ruins), and Tower (English scenery). The latter two are still being made by Spode.

Ironstone

Ironstone is a term applied to a type of semiporcelain from about 1813 to as late as 1890. From 1890 to 1898 it was called white granite; since that time it has been generally called semiporcelain. Because of its durability it was popular and made in great quantities, both in England and the United States. The beginning collector should know that much American-made Ironstone was stamped with the English coat of arms, since English china was preferred by the public of that day to American-made ware.

A great deal of the Ironstone was plain white and rather thick. Finer varieties were decorated with luster bands and designs. One of the types collected most avidly today is Blue Ironstone which has scenes and borders in blue, considerably lighter in color than the Staffordshire Old Blue.

Some Ironstone is clumsy and lacking in luster and beauty. It is, in most categories, of Victorian origin. The thinner, finer varieties are well worth collecting, especially for the person who simply must collect china but also has to watch his pocketbook.

Delft

The word Delft has come to mean blue to most people. When the Dutch potters at Delft attempted to reproduce the Chinese porcelain pieces brought home by the Dutch trading vessels, they not only reproduced the porcelain but also copied the blue.

"Old Delft" is a majolica ware or glazed earthenware, first made in Holland, then by English potters at Bristol, Liverpool, and in Staffordshire. Old Delft was perishable because of its glaze which chipped and scaled. Because of its early manufacture and rarity, it is now beyond most collectors. Occasionally, however, one finds a

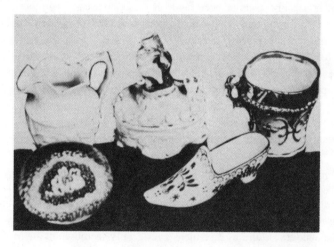

FIG. 105. A few small Victorian collectibles suitable for the what-not. A Parian pitcher, Staffordshire trinket box, china cup, Delft slipper, and paperweight.

small piece which may be hopefully called Delft. The authors have one such piece in their collection. It looks like Delft, it feels like Delft. Who knows, maybe it *is* Delft!

Lotus Ware

The authors realize that much of the material being presented is about china that is too old and too valuable to be acquired. It helps, however, to know something about the rarer things because one occasionally finds a "sleeper" in a shop which may be added to a collection for little money.

Lotus ware, however, is well within the Victorian period. It is not old or rare but certainly it is beautiful. It is really a lightweight porcelain, heavily decorated, usually all white, and characterized by its lacy filigree designs applied in raised fashion. This produces a very delicate effect which, in combination with the fine porcelain used in its manufacture, makes it very desirable indeed.

Some authorities assert, and with some justification, that Lotus ware is the finest china ever made by an American manufacturer. Knowles, Taylor and Knowles of Liverpool, Ohio, began to market it in 1893. Each piece is marked "Lotus Ware," with the name of the firm. It was modestly produced for seven years only, between 1893 and 1900. In addition, it was expensive to buy. As a consequence, there is not an abundance on the market today. Because of this fact and because of the perfection of its workmanship, Lotus ware is an excellent field for the collector who likes to acquire the unusual which might have a very bright future.

Majolica

As ordinary collectors, the writers have probably never seen a piece of *real* Italian majolica of the fifteenth or sixteenth century. This was being made in various Italian towns when America was still a wilderness and as a result is found only in museums or in the hands of wealthy collectors. There probably is good reason, however, to call the ware in antique shops majolica because the term is synonymous with faïence, a French word which is applied to all glazed earthenware.

Authorities seem to differ as to what should and should not be termed majolica, and the authors have neither the desire nor the qualifications to become embroiled in the discussion. It seems sufficient to say that the highly glazed, heavy earthenware with the browns, deep greens, pinks, and yellows, and the various shapes of plates, pitchers, etc., can be termed majolica. In view of the number of collectors of the ware, prices have become rather high. It is advisable, therefore, that the reader investigate further into the study of majolica before investing too heavily as a collector.

Gaudy Dutch

This soft-paste pottery was made with the blue under the glaze and the other colors applied over the glaze and then baked on. As a result of this method, the top colors are easily chipped off. Thus it is rather difficult to find this ware in perfect condition.

At one time it was believed that this ware was produced in Pennsylvania but most authorities now agree that it was made by English potters and shipped to America for the trade. Much of it was probably made before the War of 1812. Gaily decorated and in some variants having touches of color, it has many collectors. Like Gaudy Welsh, Adam's Red Rose, and Gaudy Ironstone, it is difficult to find, but makes worth-while collections.

Haviland

The story of Haviland is one of American aggressiveness. When, in 1839, a customer in the shop of David and Daniel Haviland in New York City asked them to match a cup that she carried, a new style of china was born. David Haviland went to Franch with the cup, searching for a pottery that could match it. The Havilands wanted French porcelain molded and decorated in the English style for the American trade!

This seemed impossible to the French potters, but after hiring an instructor to train a hundred artists in the English style, having the molds made, and finally establishing their own factory at Limoges in 1846, the Havilands started a vogue for fine dinnerware in America. Their perseverance paid off, for by 1878 they had the largest factory in the Limoges district and had made the name Haviland mean fine china.

In addition to dinner sets and teasets, they made quantities of dessert plates with fruit, marine life, water lilies, etc., for centers. This fragile china has long been a favorite with the Victorian collector. It is easily identified by the marks which varied slightly but included either the word of Haviland or the initial H. and Co.

This certainly is a field for the collector who likes fine china but who cannot afford to accumulate the rarer varieties.

Many are the collectors who search for "pattern" china, building, cup by cup, plate by plate, a complete set for use on special occasions. Mentioned previously was the Onion pattern, made in Meissen, in Holland, and by English potters. "Sprig" is another pattern which has caught the fancy of collectors. It is a delicate design and the collector of Sprig needs patience for his task. It is, however, one of the more charming patterns in china.

One of the newer collectibles is Willow ware. For many years those financially able have picked up the very old Cantonese Willow china, but in recent years more modest collectors have found that much the same pleasure and effect could be got from looking for English and Dutch Willow ware. It is surprising how difficult it is to find that, too, and how its value has increased due to the demand.

The early china was made according to a design brought from China as early as 1772 by Turner, Spode, and others. This serves as a guiding star for the more lowly collector of English ware that was turned out by Allerton and other English and Dutch potters in the nineteenth century. To build up a table service of this Willow may take years of painstaking search because, as a result of its availability, it was commonly and carelessly used. A nine-inch plate, a cup or a saucer, platter, or covered dish will usually be found in lonely seclusion in the shops.

The authors' collection now comprises service for twelve. Much of the Willow ware's interest lies in the markings on each article (a few are unmarked) and in the variations in the basic design. A single piece of Canton may serve as a basis for comparison.

The story depicted on all Willow ware is that of Koong-see, daughter of a mandarin, who fell in love with her father's secretary, Chang. When the mandarin discovered the love affair, he imprisoned his daughter in her apartments and built a high wooden fence to the edge of the river (this fence is always clearly visible). He then betrothed Koong-see to a rich viceroy named Ta-jin.

When Ta-jin arrived for the ceremony, he brought a box of fabulous jewels. During the excitement pervading the wedding preparations, Chang and Koong-see eloped to a little island where dwelt a loyal servant. There they were married. This island is at the left-hand corner of the design. On the bridge can be seen three figures: Koong-see carrying a distaff (symbol of virginity), Chang bearing Ta-jin's jewels, and the mandarin in close pursuit carrying a whip.

After their marriage, Koong-see and Chang sailed away to another little island, which they purchased with Ta-jin's jewels. Here they lived until discovered by Ta-jin, who killed Chang, whereupon Koong-see set fire to the house and perished therein.

The two doves at the top of the design represent the spirits of the two lovers, forever gazing into each other's eyes.

Whatever the variations in design, whatever the maker's mark on the back of the plate, at whatever time it was made, the blue is the same and the story it tells is ever the same.

Markings

When trying to identify a piece of china the collector, in addition to examining the biscuit, the glaze, and distinctive coloring, always looks at the bottom for marks which in many cases will help, although they are not always to be relied upon. To do this it will be necessary to have at hand one of the several excellent reference books now available. The authors have found particularly helpful a small book in pamphlet form called Crooke's *Manual of Marks* in which Mr. Crooke gives distinctive marks of German, English, French, and Dutch potters, to name but a few, and at the end some of the American potters' marks.

Another book, *The Handbook of Old Pottery and Porcelain Marks* by C. Jordan Thorn includes 4,000 marks. This book is especially valuable to the small collector because it includes a section on United States markings of Victorian times.

Many hours of study will be necessary to familiarize oneself with the outstanding marks and constant reference will be necessary to determine approximate dates. The marks on each type of china changed constantly, varying from year to year. For example, the famous crossed swords of Meissen (or Dresden) have been used from 1721 to the present time. But a large number of other potteries copied the mark. Anyone who assumes that the crossed swords

FIG. 106. The better class of collectibles in Rudolstadt, Meissen, and Dresden. Top left. Rudolstadt. Large center figure, Meissen. Top right, Dresden. (Courtesy Olde Lamps, Inc., Buffalo, N. Y.)

guarantee the article upon which they are found to be Meissen must be considered naïve.

The authors realize that much of the material covered in the above-mentioned books is far too old to be considered Victorian and far too expensive for modest collectors but, as has been said, occasionally one finds a "sleeper," and if some knowledge of its marks has been acquired, the collector can identify and buy it.

As Mr. Crooke points out, if a piece is unmarked it may still be good. If the piece is good, and the price is low, it should be bought and then an attempt made to identify it by matching it with similar marked pieces. Workmen were occasionally careless and forgot to put their distinguishing mark on good pieces of china or pottery.

CHAPTER XII

Glassware

IN GENERAL, the glass market, in antiques and near-antiques, is a dangerous one for the novice. For one thing, many of the newer dealers are not certain what they are selling, and the influx of clever reproductions bearing the prices of genuine articles has now reached a point where only the most expert guidance can be trusted. Naturally those engaged in the manufacture of reproductions do not bother with the late nineteenth century run-of-the-mill pressed glass. There is little or no incentive in reproducing dollar butter dishes or two-dollar compotes.

It is only when the price of an item reaches beyond the ten-dollar level that the manufacturer begins to smell juicy profit. At this point he aims to bag easy, ignorant game and he has to date had very little trouble in so doing. Some cleverly produced reproductions will make even an expert use his "specs"; and the poor amateur can do little but hazard a guess or take the advice of a dealer who may know little more than he or who, on the other hand, knows full well that his merchandise is as modern as television.

The subject of glassware is so vast, so confusing, and so filled with subtleties that this short treatment can do little more than help the novice skirt the pitfalls. He must do a great deal of reading, handle and fondle a great amount of glass, acquaint himself with the various patterns, and, above all, have the oft-repeated advantage of consultation with experts before he trusts himself with the purchase of really expensive items. Much benefit can be gained from trips to museums that contain collections of fine old nineteenth century glass, if the museums are within reasonable distance.

Many are the new arrivals among the collectors of Americana who seek some sort of easy, sugar-coated short cut to the positive identification of glassware. Let it be said here and now that no such short cut exists. Nothing can take the place of laboriously and patiently accumulated experience over a period of years. It is often amusing in the extreme to see a newcomer pick up a piece of glassware and knowingly strike it with his knuckle to see if it will ring. Ringing more often than not is meaningless as far as identification

Fig. 107. A late fleur-de-leis pattern in flint glass which demonstrates the brilliancy even of late flint produced by the old-line companies in the 1870's and 1880's.

is concerned. Of course, many think that the louder and truer the ring the finer the quality of the glass. It should then follow that the glass that rings is the rarer glass. The truth is that all good flint glass rings, and flint glass is very common even in its good form.

Another thing not often considered by people who practice this worthless test is that the physical shape of a piece of glassware affects the frequency of the emitted sound as well as the glass itself. Often these wiseacres who make such on-the-spot tests are serenely unconscious of the presence of a really valuable piece of glass because when struck it produces only a dull, unromantic thud. Sometimes, as in the case of early-versus-late Sandwich milk glass, the

209

ring test may have some meaning. The early variety rings better than the later stuff. In a few other cases the ring may have a certain meaning for the experts, but on the whole it is a poor guide for the beginner. Of course, the shyster type of dealer likes to demonstrate glass that rings well, and many a sale has been consummated with the help of such spurious evidence of quality.

One of the most reliable tests for either clear or colored glass is its cast: its appearance in good light and the way in which light is transmitted through it. This is the most important professional

Fig. 108. Showing the difference between late Hobnail (left) and Thousand Eye (right).

means of positive identification and even this is not wholly reliable because of the very minute differences in the composition of the glassware produced by some factories. Naturally the identification mentioned above can be made only after long association with the field. When the matter of design and pattern is added to cast, color, and feel, one has included all of the reliable methods of identifying the various wares. It is a vast and confusing field where even the top experts often tread lightly.

The following pages are in no sense offered as anything but a crude guide; a bare introduction to a vast subject requiring, in many of its phases, a lifetime of study.

While this is no place to discuss the techniques of glass composition or glass manufacture, the collector will add much pleasure to the hobby of collecting if he will acquaint himself with the general practices used in the craft, both early and late. For the serious collector making substantial investments in early Sandwich glass this is, of course, a "must." For practical reasons, one should be able to distinguish between blown, blown-mold, and pressed glass.

Fig. 109. Some of the more common patterns in glass, produced in the late 1880's.

Such distinctions often have a great deal to do with rarities vs. more ordinary or less rare pieces.

These important data may very pleasantly be absorbed by a reading of either the McKearins' very scholarly work entitled *American Glass* (available in most libraries) or the various and excellent works of Ruth Webb Lee. It is of course best to read all of the works of these authors. One can have only the greatest admiration for these thorough scholars, whose laborious researches extend over long periods of years and who have added so much accurate knowledge to a long-neglected field of absorbing Americana. Especially interesting is the record of the early pioneer in pressed glass, Deming Jarves; and of the New England Glass Works and the Boston and Sandwich Company, whose histories begin in the year 1818.

From the busy molds of these pioneer concerns came the most exquisite examples of flint glass in pattern form. As an instance, among the most eagerly sought items of the present day one might mention the delightful cup plates in what is now generally called Lacy Sandwich. Especially desirable are the historical cup plates such as the Stamped Eagle, Fort Meigs, Log Cabin, Benjamin Harrison, Henry Clay, Bunker Hill, Benjamin Franklin, etc.

Fig. 110. Milk white glass plates of the type popular during the late 1870's and 1880's. One of the very popular collectibles of the present time. Most modern reproductions of this ware are crude and lifeless.

The genius of this work lay not only in a certain naïveté of design but, still more to be admired, in its effect on light, the delicate refractions and reflections produced. If the reader has never seen one of the finer examples of a Lacy Sandwich cup plate, let him imagine a greatly magnified snowflake in the sunlight. Some day an expert in optics will take the trouble to discover how those early designers at Sandwich became masters in the control of the sunbeam and of its antics as it passed through what was once but an unromantic blob of hot plastic so as to reach the eye. All of this magic was produced from ordinary clear flint or crystal glass.

One must not, however, be naïve enough to think that specimens of this type are to be found in every antique shop. Although millions of these must have been made (this manufacture perhaps extended into the 1860's) time has taken a terrific and tragic toll. So it is, too, with the other pressed-glass articles of earlier date: bowls, plates, compotes, salts, sugars, creamers, and the like. Oh, for the treasures that great-grandmother thought nothing of buying for a few pennies! Many of them are now worth a dollar for every penny she spent.

Fig. 111. A type of Thumb Print ware made during the 1870's. All Thumb Print patterns are popular.

All pressed glass, however, was not clear flint glass although by far the greatest mass of it was clear. Some was milk white, some blue, some opalescent, etc. Nor, as the authorities point out, was all pressed glass Sandwich, nor all Sandwich glass pressed. Sandwich, guided by the genius of Jarves, also produced glassware so much in the manner of the fabulous Baron von Stiegel (late eighteenth century) that present-day authorities have great difficulty distinguishing between the two, a warning to neophytes who are inclined to purchase specimens offered as Stiegel without seeking expert opinion. The high price asked for true Stiegel would warrant such caution.

Jarves did not develop his lacy glass until the 1830's but when it did arrive it so quickly captivated the public that it came forth from his presses in a great crystal flood and continued to do so for many years. Although millions of dollars worth, at present-day prices, was either willfully destroyed or lost by accident, a considerable mass of it survived. Today it brings high prices although . it is neither scarce nor rare. This is due, simply to the large number of collectors of it, including those who once looked down their expert noses at it. Although a great deal of the early Sandwich glass is tucked away in collectors' cupboards, those who still wish to

FIG. 112. Maple Leaf pattern of the 1880's.

collect it are not advised to wait for a crack in the price structure of the market for it. Many who own such collections would rather put cardboard in the bottoms of their shoes than to part with even a single piece, a resolve appreciated by those who have a true love for crystal glass in one of its finest forms.

Unfortunately the difficulties of the newly arrived collector of glass are increased somewhat by too loose a usage of the word Sandwich, which in some minds is almost synonymous with pressed glass. The Boston and Sandwich Glass Company by no means had a monopoly on pressed or even lacy glass. The New England Glass Company, organized in 1818 (one of the organizers was Jarves who retired from the concern in 1825 to organize what later became the Boston and Sandwich Company) was a brisk competitor, as were others, especially in Pittsburgh and Ohio. Identification of the products of the various companies is made possible largely through the designs used in their various wares and not through detectable (especially for amateurs!) differences in manufacturing methods or the nature of the glass used, all of it being a fine form of flint. Again the authors advise the reader to go to the books already mentioned if he is to prepare himself for the collection of anything but the late nineteenth century ware, of which more later. To repeat, there is no short cut to an understanding of the pressed glass

Fig. 113. The very popular collectible: Pleat and Panel. Also one of the heavily reproduced patterns.

made between the 1820's and the 1860's. It is easy enough to purchase as true Sandwich a dolphin pressed-glass candleholder made by McKee and Brothers at Pittsburgh in the 1860's and sold at $6.00 a dozen. The difference is in the base, but the purchaser must be armed with facts to know such things.

Especially desirable are some of the beautiful specimens of what is known as cased or overlay glass appearing in compotes, lamps, vases, decanters, etc. Authorities claim that this beautiful ware was probably not produced in this country before 1840. The top of the vogue for it came in the early 1860's. It is not in any sense rare but most desirable, and the large number of collectors has resulted in a very thin and lively market for it. This ware was produced from two layers of colored glass the outer layer being cut through in design to reveal the inner layer.

To understand the bulk of the pattern glass market and the average collector in that field, one must turn the pages of American glass-making history to the last half of the nineteenth century. As was invariably the case with all things, high quality began to disappear and designs began to deteriorate. Even the glass industry was not left untouched by the poisonous Eastlake mode. For it, too, this

Fig. 114. A variation of the Maple Leaf pattern with opalescent rim. Probably as late as the 1890's.

was the era of mass production when thousands of tons of the fiery liquid were drained from the furnaces to create all manner of tableware. Millions of pieces have survived. It is with this stuff largely that the modern collector has gorged himself.

This is not to say that it was not good glass, although low in price, low enough indeed to be sold first by the "variety stores" of the times and later by the early Woolworth stores. It had "life" too; it was clear and sparkling. Modern reproductions of these designs, now such a bane to the newcomer, are in most cases rather sad in comparison; the cruder of it would seem to have been made from milk bottle stock. Some, however, is good enough to stump the experts, unless they stop to give it a very close examination. So rampant and unfair has this traffic become that Ruth Webb Lee, the noted authority, has issued an invaluable little book on the subject. Among known reproductions now on the market, some of them openly and some of them surreptitiously offered as the genuine McCoy, she lists the following, all of them popular patterns:

1. Westward Ho goblets, sauce dishes, and lamps, the latter never having been made originally. The blue goblets now being offered in this pattern were never before made in this color either

2. Lion goblets, sugar bowls, creamers, sauce dishes, celery vases, bread plates, egg cups, two sizes of compotes

3. Three-Face goblets, cordials, champagne, etc.

4. Horn of Plenty tumblers, of both amber and crystal glass

5. Pineapple wineglasses and goblets

6. Tulip wineglasses

7. Cherry goblets

8. Panelled Grape in all varieties of form

9. Dewdrop With Star in form of seven-inch plate, salts, etc.

10. Ivy in Snow in every original form

11. Baltimore Pear in form of sugar bowl, sauces, etc.

12. Moon and Star goblets

13. Rose in Snow goblets and large plates, compotes, etc.

14. Hobnail is being produced in large quantities and in a wide variety of forms. This is the most popular of all reproduced patterns

15. Dew and Raindrop goblets, sherbet cups, and cordials

16. Daisy and Button in round and square plates, hats, and many other forms

17. Roman Rosette goblets

18. Thousand Eye goblets in both clear and colored glass

19. Shell and Tassel goblets

20. Milk white "S" plates

21. Wildflower goblets, clear and colored; square plates, clear and apple green.

The field in pattern glass is so vast and the number of patterns available so great that every collector can find something that will appeal to his or her fancy. It can easily happen, too, that sooner or later a fickle public may suddenly gravitate toward one of the heretofore neglected departments of American glass. How nice it would then be to be caught with a good lot of it taken in at low prices! That has happened before, in the case of almost all of the now-most-popular ten. An evening spent with one or more of the good glass books mentioned previously, wherein hundreds of photographs and

Fig. 115. Thumb Print celery (left), Deer and Pine Tree (middle), and Daisy and Button (right). All three of these patterns are among the most popular ten collectibles of the present time. Courtesy Mrs. Penn Perkins.

drawings of Late American pressed glass are shown, may help one to pick a winner.

Late American colored and novelty glass in all forms is extremely popular with American collectors. Indeed during the past few years, it has been literally swept off the market. What remains demands fabulous prices and has long since lost all semblance of representing attractive investments. What is more, by far the larger percentage of the colored glass articles being sought were produced (many of them in great volume) during the last twenty years of the nineteenth century, and they not only have no right to the word antique but they do not in any sense deserve the prices they bring.

As an example let us take Amberina ware, once produced by the New England Glass Company, having been introduced by it in 1883. This glass resulted from a fluke in the production of ruby glassware in which the metal gold was involved. At first Amberina, so named by Edward D. Libbey, amounted only to imperfect ruby.

Fig. 116. Lion pattern, (middle) very late variation of the Loop and Fan pattern, and (right) a specimen of the very popular Bellflower pattern. Courtesy Mrs. Penn Perkins.

At any rate, upon its introduction the public purchased it almost as fast as it could be made. It appeared in many forms; water pitchers, glasses, berry sets, pickle casters, finger bowls, etc.

About the same time there also appeared on the market spangled glassware, pomona glass, rose ware (beautifully blended tints), Agata, cranberry, etc. All of these are in short supply and great demand today. It is, nevertheless, very fortunate that this important and experimental period of glassware Americana will be preserved by representative collections. The movement and interest itself is entirely laudable.

Certain types of glassware require very little experience for reliable identification. Bristol may be taken as an example; Victorian Bristol, that is. The early Bristol produced in England during the eighteenth century is not apt to be found in the average antique shop. During the latter part of the nineteenth century, however, a modified Bristol formula was widely used in France, Bohemia, Eng-

Fig. 117. Opalescent Coin Spot water pitcher in blue. Although once given away as premiums to holders of coupons taken from baking soda packages, these pitchers demand good prices today.

land, Holland, and the United States for the production of Victorian bric-a-brac. This type of Bristol has a highly glossed surface, extremely smooth to the touch, and is opaque, appearing in a wide range of colors and shades. It is also found in the form of what has become known as "cased glass," which is one color on the outside and another on the inside.

The Bohemian stuff, above all, is rather easy to identify because of its gay nature, much of it being decorated with enamel. The French version of Bristol, far more scarce, is characterized by decoration; while the American article, in far better supply, assumes a wide variety of form and color, vases being the most popular. A common form of vase is that with rose-colored lining, enamelled floral decoration, and ruffled top. On the whole, it will be found that the more ornate forms such as the ruffled edge were late. During the 1880's, Bristol ware had crimped and fluted edges. As a general rule the earlier ware was a little more sedate. It is also well to ·note that Bristol vases were originally sold in pairs and should be so purchased whenever possible.

During the latter part of the 1880's, still another form of ornamental glass violently pushed its way into the American market and remained "put" for a ten-year period. This was satin glass, popular with collectors to a point where it commands prices considerably out of line with its availability. Produced in a wide variety of shades and colors and with rather delightful bleeding effects, it also assumed a wide variety of forms, the well-known spherical rose bowl with crimped edge being the most popular. Aside from rose bowls, there were also vases, drinking glasses, butters, creamers, sugars, bonbonnières, etc. Originally this form of glassware was introduced by the Phoenix Glass Company of Pittsburgh, Pennsylvania, as mother-of-pearl satin glass. The relationship between the feel and texture of pearl and satin glass is close. Satin glass, while not expensive, is truly beautiful.

Among the less abundant (by far) forms of ornamental glassware made in America we find favrile first produced by the brilliant artist, Louis Comfort Tiffany, and introduced by him in 1893. It is characterized chiefly by its wide forms of iridescence, ranging from somber to very light tones. It made its appearance in the form of vases, lamp shades, vanity boxes, candlesticks, compotes, teapots, trays, bonbonnières, etc. It would appear that the collector of Tiffany, especially the rarer items, should not be in too great a hurry to dispose of his hoard providing his collection has been assembled with care and with an eye to reasonable price. Especially fortunate are those who assembled their collections before the urge to collect became so widespread.

In years gone by, much of America's ornamental glassware was imported from the glass-making Bohemians, who excelled in certain forms, especially ruby ware. During the latter part of the nineteenth century tremendous quantities of this ware were sold by our shops, but the finer specimens of the craft are too good to be lightly discounted. They will perhaps maintain their value as well as anything

FIG. 118. (Left) An early Waffle and Thumb Print decanter and (right) Ashburton type of decanter with blown stopper. Both represent types of the better pattern glass coming from the Mid-Victorian period.

over the coming years. Especially is this true of such things as lusters, or spill vases, overlay decanters, toilet water bottles, and the like. Many of the finer decanters sold in this country during the 1860's were of ruby glass.

On the other hand, American ruby is not so good. As a matter of fact, it is patently inferior to the Bohemian product in most cases; produced by different methods, cheaper methods, to be exact.

Both the real stuff and the American substitute appeared in the form of water pitchers and glasses, sugar bowls, plates, candy trays, souvenir mugs (Niagara Falls as late as 1910), butter dishes, teacups with saucers, etc.

Not only is the American ruby glass itself inferior, but the coloring as well. As a matter of fact, the coloring was a cheap substitute offered no doubt to take advantage of the brisk market for the finer imported ware, honestly manufactured in the best traditions of Bohemian craftsmanship.

Fig. 119. (Left) Satin glass vase (1890's), majolica leaf dish (middle, and right) a late American Bristol vase with enamelled decorations.

Inasmuch as ruby ware is being aggressively sought today and demands prices far above its original cost, the collector must use caution if he wishes to assemble a collection beyond a few pieces. It behooves him to be able at least to distinguish between the inferior product of America and the vastly superior product of Bohemia. Fortunately for such collectors, the American product is marked by glaring crudities.

For one thing, the Americans did not match the deep, uniform ruby shade produced by the Bohemians nor did they match the fine quality of glass in which the shade was produced. Holding a Bohemian water tumbler up to the light of a window along with the cheaper American product will quickly convince one of the great inferiority of the American ware. It has a smoky or muddy-brown-

FIG. 120. One of the finer, earlier, and rarer Bohemian lusters or spill vases with painted medallions. Lusters of lesser grandeur are being imported from Czechoslovakia today. Such things came in pairs. Courtesy Olde Lamps, Inc., Buffalo, N. Y.

red cast to it when viewed through transmitted light, differing from the clear rich tone of Bohemian red. Yet despite this manifest difference, many ignorant and unscrupulous antique dealers during the past few years have grouped all of this ware together, making no distinction between the two in price. Whereas the Bohemian product was imperishable in point of color, the American product (made in Pittsburgh, most of it), whose color was produced by a fired-in surface treatment, could be scratched and removed readily.

And then there is cranberry glass! One can almost hear the ladies sigh at the mere mention of the word. That which was Montgomery Ward's mediocrity in their 1895 catalogue has become one of today's choicest collectibles. Mail-order houses and variety stores were once

Fig. 121. Among the rarer and finer glass-ware collectibles imported from Bohemia during the Mid-Victorian period. This center bowl is part of a cobalt blue and white table set. Courtesy Olde Lamps, Inc., Buffalo, N. Y.

happy to receive less than five dollars for a berry bowl and a dozen sauces but one shudders at the prices asked for such a set today. Yes, it *is* pretty in transmitted light, it *is* dainty and all that, but as far as the present writers are concerned let the reader keep a dozen tumblers, a berry set, or a water pitcher and give them in exchange just one of Jarves' early Lacy Sandwich cup plates!

Heavy investments in cranberry (and they can be heavy!) are somewhat dangerous. How long this unreasonable market will last no one knows, what with a fickle public and with presentable reproductions flooding the market. Surely sounder investments may be made in glassware.

If a modern collector of late Victorian novelty glassware or ornamental glassware with ample funds wishes to depart from collecting norms, let him consider peachblow or Burmese and let him also become reconciled to the fact that he will have to travel far and wide over a period of years to gather a representative collection. However, such a venture might well pay off over the years. Certainly an investment in such ware, if carefully made, would be much sounder than investments in more common pieces. Some day much of the latter, now hoarded on window shelves and in china closets, will come back to market and the effect may well be disastrous. The supply is too big to be safe.

Also to be considered is the pressed colored glass of the late nineteenth century; vaseline, blue, green, amethyst, etc. The volume was not as great as that of crystal or flint glass but still a great deal of it was produced. It is good, it is pretty, and the long-term market may hold up. Whatever the reader may choose to collect, the authors wish him luck and, above all, that sort of solid relaxation that so many busy people need these days. The hobby of collecting can be an investment in health, too.

Between 1870 and 1890 several hundred patterns and designs were employed by the many glass concerns of the United States. By far the largest percentage of these were pretty bad, artistically speaking. The modern collectors have in a manner exercised their collective judgment in rejecting most of the specimens as not desirable collectibles, for it is found that the demand for ten of the patterns far outstrips the demand for the rest of the stuff. It is now generally conceded that the following patterns come first in the esteem of the majority of collectors: Bellflower, Horn of Plenty, Rose in Snow, Wildflower, Thousand Eye, Three-Face, Lion, Westward-Ho, Daisy and Button, and Milk White Blackberry, the latter an opaque glass often just called Milk Glass.

It was supposed to have been a part of the code of ethics of the glassmakers of the time that patterns brought out by one concern might not be copied by another without written permission; but there were so many violations, especially by the lesser lights, that one cannot be too sure that his treasure was made by such-and-such company even though that company originated the pattern.

FIG. 122. A pair of fine old crystal glass bottles of the Civil War period. (Courtesy Olde Lamps, Inc., Buffalo, N. Y.)

A number of the popular patterns named above are illustrated in the photographs of this book. All enjoy a brisk market and brisk markets are usually high markets. However, it can well be that the new collector will find among the less popular patterns one which will suit his fancy and provide great pleasure for him.

227

CHAPTER XIII

Silver, Pewter, and Britannia Ware

LEAST cursed by the fancies and foibles of the early and mid-Victorians is the silver, pewter, Britannia and Sheffield ware made between the years of 1835 and 1865. These years as a whole saw the last of the honest, patient craftsmanship produced by the individual worker; unaided by the machine, except, perhaps, for the spinner's lathe. A great deal of the silver hollow-ware produced between 1840 and 1860 was in good taste and much of it remains uncollected today, so preoccupied have the connoisseurs been in collecting the stuff made during the eighteenth century. However, the day for avid accumulation of Early Victorian ware in all of the metals, silver, pewter, Britannia, and Sheffield cannot be far off, and many smart people have for a number of years been quietly picking up the best of it at relatively low prices. A great deal of it still remains to be found, however.

That much individually made silverware was produced during early and mid-Victorian times there can be no doubt. It is said that during the 1840's some 2,500 silversmiths were at work in the cities and towns of the United States. Their labors and their products, however, remain one of the unwritten chapters of Americana, shame that it is. The touch mark (each worker had a marking tool which was applied to his finished pieces, a practice started in England by law several centuries before Victorian times) of the meanest of the eighteenth century pewterers and silversmiths is known and recorded by the experts, while that of many of even the best of the Victorian workers is unknown. One can anticipate the scramble, come the day when these fellows are "discovered" and the experts set about giving them their due.

Prior to 1850, when electroplated ware began to reach the market, practically all good silverware in any form, sold as such and made by local silversmiths, was of coin silver. This is not pure silver, as many think. As a matter of fact, one would not wish to have a piece of silverware made of pure silver, so soft is the metal. What is known as "fine" silver is 999/1000 pure and was never used by the ware-makers.

There is really very little difference between sterling silver (a very old formula going back to the early history of England) and coin silver, as the latter term is used in connection with the hand-made ware of early Victorian times. Coin silver was the name given the alloy formula used by the United States Mint. Such silver was 900/1000 fine or 9/10 pure, ten per cent of copper being added for strength. Sterling boasted of a purity amounting to 925/1000. Sterling on the whole, however, was not available to Victorian silversmiths and most of their excellent ware was of coin silver. Many were the Victorian housewives of the middle class who saved their silver dollars and carried them to the local silversmith with an order that they be used to make a few pieces: perhaps spoons, forks, a "sugar" and "creamer" or a tray. The coins were melted, rolled out into a sheet, and so the work began, much of it to eventuate in fine old pieces some of which owe no apologies to any of the eighteenth century boys.

Such fine silverware was made well into the 1860's and much of it is still about in every form and at prices that will one day appear ridiculously low. Often these writers have been able to purchase beautifully made coin-silver spoons for as little as one dollar each, sometimes less. They are thin, well shaped, and usually plain. Practically all have touch marks or once had them. Some silversmiths of this era simply stamped their names on the back of the spoon handle or on the bottom of hollow-ware. Others stamped their names or initials together with a star, a cross, or other symbol. Some ware was engraved with the purchaser's initials, some was not.

Fig. 123. Mid-Victorian tableware as advertised by Rogers Brothers Manufacturing Company, during the late Mid-Victorian period. In all probability Britannia ware with silver plate.

Other decoration was accomplished by chasing, molding, embossing, or stamping. However, the silversmiths of Victorian times usually engraved their decoration, and on the whole it was passable work, much of it being on a par with anything that eighteenth century fellows did and some of it being a great deal better than the best that the eighteenth century had to offer.

After experimenting for several years with the new English process for silver-plating electrochemically, the Rogers brothers, William, Asa, and Simeon, introduced their electroplated product (first in the form of spoons) in 1847. The preliminary work of experimentation had been done at Number 4 State Street, Hartford, Connecticut, the inspiration for it coming no doubt from an article dealing with the patent of the Englishman, Elkington, which had appeared in the publication of the Franklin Institute at Philadelphia. The first silver-plated ware produced by the Rogers brothers in 1847 had as its basic metal either steel or an alloy known as German silver, or nickel silver as it is now called. The mixture is a combination of copper, nickel, and zinc, about two-thirds of the former and varying proportions of the latter two metals. Although called German silver, the alloy is believed to have been first used in China. Some of the cheaper tableware produced before the introduction of silver-plating was of German silver, when it was not made of iron or low-grade steel with bone or wooden handles. Cheap spoons of pewter were also used in these times, and many of the Midwest farmers of the Early Victorian period cast their own pewter spoons in a soapstone mold. Starting out with a few pounds of pewter and by saving each broken spoon for remelting, even a large family could make such a small supply last for a good many years.

Properly to trace and understand the story behind the early plated hollow-ware, one must go back to the earlier part of the nineteenth century to pick up the story of pewter and Britannia ware, the latter made of a relatively soft metal closely akin to pewter. As might be known, pewter itself goes back to a distant point in European and American history.

Most beginners believe that pewter is practically all lead when as

FIG. 124. Some of the Late Victorian silverware, much of which was in the Eastlake mode. The contraption in the lower right hand corner was called an ice cream stand.

a matter of fact it is mostly tin. This, however, is not to be confused with tinware which was made of sheet iron that had been dipped into hot tin for reasons of appearance and, more important still, for reasons of providing an antirust surface. Pewter is usually a tin-lead alloy. Some pewter was also of a better grade tin-copper or tin-brass alloy. The various pewter alloys were used for various purposes. Pewter containing forty per cent of lead was used in making the cheaper articles and was known as "black metal."

Many individual pewterers continued in business during the early years of the nineteenth century, but were gradually replaced by the small factory, which used improved methods of manufacture but only as these methods increased the production. Certainly they added nothing to the quality of the workmanship. Whereas the individual pewterer used his personal touch mark, much of the factory-made stuff was minus this identification. Aside from spoons, pewter ware appeared in the form of plates, platters, tea- and coffee-

FIG. 125. The vogue in table hollowware during the 1870's and 1880's. Fortunately the vogue for this ugly stuff among collectors is nil, although in its day such silverware was made by such fine old companies as Reed and Barton. (Courtesy Reed and Barton)

pots, trays, porringers, pitchers, etc. Obviously the metal was not of the sort that could be employed for cutlery. Handmade pewter ware was fashioned by hammering, casting in molds, or by a combination of both. Some was spun from a sheet on a spinning lathe. Burnishing was also accomplished on a lathe.

By 1840, true pewter ware made for sale in the small shops had practically disappeared. The reason for this gradual snuffing out of an ancient craft had become evident many years before when in England there appeared a new pewter-like alloy called Britannia metal. Still another development that helped to spell the doom of old-formula pewter was the rather acceptable and cheap chinaware that began to appear during the first quarter of the nineteenth century. Pressed glass, too, in newer and cheaper forms, might have had a great deal to do with the passing of pewter.

Really Britannia metal was a first cousin of pewter, being rich in added copper and antimony. No lead was used and therefore a brighter and more silver-like color was achieved. Later came white metal which was composed of tin, copper, lead, antimony, and bismuth. The larger the amounts of tin used in these alloys, the greater the similarity of the metal's appearance to its superior, silver.

Fig. 126. Early Britannia ware teapots made by Babbit, Crossman and Company (1827) parent company of Reed and Barton. (Courtesy Reed and Barton)

Several concerns began to manufacture Britannia hollow-ware in the 1820's before true pewter had yet given up the ghost. One such manufacturer was Babbitt, Crossman and Company, forerunner of the fine old New England company of Reed and Barton, who made Britannia teapots. Probably the first Britannia metal to bear the famous Reed and Barton stamp was produced in 1846.

Come 1835, a relatively large number of people, some of them former pewterers, were in the Britannia business. A great deal of this business was in Meriden, Connecticut, town and vicinity. It was there that Ashbil Griswold started as a pewterer in 1808 and, after having taken in a partner in 1830, became one of the leading manufacturers of Britannia ware in the United States, employing many men in his factory. The carts of the Yankee peddlers were heavy with Griswold's Britannia ware when they left Meriden in those days, each piece with his famous eagle touch mark on its bottom. It was this concern that later merged with the Rogers brothers to form the early foundation upon which the now famous International Silver Company, still of the same address, was to be built.

Come the 1850's Connecticut teemed with manufacturers of Britannia ware. Nor were they confined to this state, birthplace of the

FIG. 127. Some Mid-Victorian tableware of silver-plated Britannia metal, copper, and brass. This is the sort of inexpensive ware found today which adds an authentic Victorian note to any table.

craft. More and better molds were made as production quickened. Fabrication of molded parts into complete articles was facilitated by the ease with which Britannia ware was soldered. The list of articles was long and impressive and by no means limited to tableware. There were coffeepots, teapots, pitchers, caster frames, lamps for fluid or lard, candlesticks, ladles, sugars and creamers, slop bowls, mugs, cups, cigar lighters, liquor shakers, decanter stoppers, bitters tubes, tumblers, tobacco boxes, spittoons, toy cups, handles, shaving boxes, sewing birds, and many other items.

In the meantime the Rogers brothers and others, but the Rogers brothers in particular, had made progress in the new art of electroplating silver, and in 1855 the Meriden Britannia Company, a merger set up a few years before, introduced silver-plated hollow-ware of Britannia metal. Although Britannia ware had originally gained favor over true pewter because it was more easily polished and scoured by housewives, the new silver-plated ware with its truly silver sheen very quickly caught the public fancy.

Many hollow-ware pieces of Britannia were offered either plain or in silver plate. It was during this year, 1855, that the Meriden

Fig. 128. Mid-Victorian silver-plated candelabra and Britannia ware teaset with tray.

Britannia Company alone catalogued no less than 104 different dinner casters, bad news indeed for the collector of Victorian table-ware who would assemble a complete representation of such things. These were still the days of the Yankee peddlers and many were the caster sets or Britannia water pitchers traded for a bag of goose feathers or a firkin of butter. And so goes the story of early Bri-tannia hollow-ware, plated and unplated. Much of it was well designed, all things considered, particularly the fact that it was relatively cheap and intended for middle-class trade.

As this chapter is being written, the authors have before them one of the catalogues of the Rogers Brothers Manufacturing Company as of 1855. In shape at least the silver-plated hollow-ware of that time followed closely the product of the late eighteenth century's sainted craftsmen. It was cursed with more ornamentation than was needed, however.

This ware is still about today, but not too easy to find in usable condition or in such condition as to be available for complete restoration without a great deal of expense, silver-plating costs being what

FIG. 129. Some of the earlier unplated Britannia ware of the type often taken for pewter by amateurs. Made by Rogers Brothers. (Courtesy International Silver Company)

they are at the present time. In view of this, one should by no means pay a great deal for old Britannia teasets in need of replating. Britannia ware held on for many years, and a modification of the same alloy now called white metal is still used. However, in later Victorian times and as metal-working machines and techniques improved, silver-plated brass and copper hollow-ware also appeared.

Sheffield plate was originated in eighteenth century England to supply mediocre grandeur to those who could not afford sterling goods. It also appeared on the Victorian scene in both English and (later) American forms, the English having supplied much of it for the American trade between 1790 and 1850. This is *plated silverware* which is not to be confused with *silver-plated ware*, the latter being

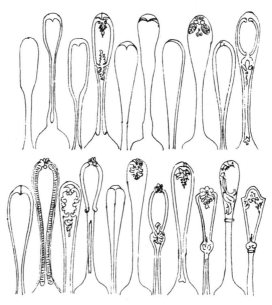

FIG. 130. Early, Mid- and Late Victorian spoon patterns produced by Rogers Brothers but indicative of the changing styles in general. (Top row from left to right) Plain, 1847; threaded, 1847; tipped, 1847; Olive, 1848; Antique, 1849; Fiddle, 1850; Windsor, 1850; Silver, 1850; French oval, 1850; Tuscan, 1852. (Lower row from left to right) Oval, 1855; Beaded, 1855; St. Charles, 1855; Gothic, 1860; Spanish, 1860; Shell, 1860; Roman, 1865; Ivy, 1870; Persian, 1871; Lily, 1872; and Princess, 1874.

electroplated whereas Sheffield plate consisted of thin coverings of sheet silver over copper, the silver being applied by a thermo-mechanical process wherein the silver was attached to the copper surface by a sort of fusing or welding. On the whole, the silver of Sheffield plate was thicker than that produced by silver electroplating, which rarely exceeded .001 inch in thickness and was much thinner on cheaper stuff.

A great deal of beautifully executed Sheffield plate in hollow- and flatware forms reached Victorian America and this enjoys a very good market today, especially the older pieces. Much of it was produced by craftsmen of great skill. During the last half of the nineteenth century, a great deal of American-made stuff reached the market. It was, with few exceptions, distinctly inferior to the British ware.

If one contemplates the putting together of a collection of good Victorian Sheffield, one should by no means set out upon the venture without first preparing oneself by reading the literature available on the subject. Otherwise a collection may be extremely costly both in money and disappointment.

After 1870, tableware in all of its forms began to suffer from the infectious Charles Eastlake ideas, and the decline in taste was precipitous and disastrous. Not a single graceful line or anything but gawky form appeared in the manufactured articles that took up the Eastlake Gothic motifs. Furniture was having its nightmare era, and tableware joined in with gusto.

As a final word, it may be said that the problem of supplying authentic Early or Mid-Victorian atmosphere to the dining table is a relatively easy one. One still finds kicking about in the antique shops shabby teasets and other hollow-ware coming from mid-Victorian times, and as likely as not in Britannia metal. They may be had for a few dollars and they should be purchased for replating, but not before a careful examination is made for holes, broken handles, deeply pitted spots where excessive corrosion has set in, and for dents beyond the superficial. Let no antique dealer volunteer the advice that deep dents can easily be ironed out, that handles can easily be soldered or welded into place, or that deeply corroded spots can by some magic be repaired. This is not true even if one could find a local craftsman who might be skilled in such work. Let no amateur attempt to weld or solder a handle back on a Britannia ware pot lest he melt himself into a pretty mess. This alloy has a low

CHASED ICE PITCHER.　　　　CHASED URN.

REVOLVING WINE STAND.　　CASTOR.　　GOBLET.

BUTTER DISH.　　SYRUP CUP.

FIG. 131. Silverware made during 1868. This was badly designed from an artistic viewpoint but not nearly as badly as that which followed a few years later.

melting point, and ordinary procedures of soldering are likely quickly to precipitate a peck of real trouble. The same holds for methods that might be applied in remedying corrosion, and only a real craftsman can iron out a deep dent to the point of complete obliteration.

If a set of ware is in prime condition and the would-be purchaser is satisfied with the design, then let him buy it and have it replated by a reliable electroplater specializing in this work and one equipped with the special wheels and buffing compounds intended only for silver. The cost will be high, from $25 to $50 for the larger and more complicated outfits, but thereafter one will have something of real beauty from which a great deal of satisfaction may be derived. Too much emphasis cannot be placed on the necessity of taking such repair jobs to reliable specialists: electroplating houses devoted exclusively to such work or those having special departments run by experts.

The plate itself does not need to be thick (.001 inch will do) but it needs to be of *uniform* thickness so that spots will not polish off prematurely. This matter of thickness and uniformity must rest entirely with the reputation of the plater and his desire to preserve that reputation.

An added touch of elegance can be provided on some hollow-ware (creamers and sugars, for instance) without too much additional cost through covering of the inside with electrodeposited gold. All good platers have gold baths, and only the slightest covering of this metal is needed to provide a lasting surface of great beauty.

INDEX

Adam, brothers, 46
Ambrotypes, 187
American Pioneer Arts and Artists,
   Carl Drepperd, 185
American Primitive Painting, Jean
   Lipman, 185

Bed,
   Belter, 132
   plywood, 132
   Eastlake, 133, 134
   four-poster, pineapple finials, 129
   Jenny Lind, 130
   Late American Empire, 127
   scroll, 131
   sleigh, 130, 131
   turned spindle, 129
Belleek, 192, 198
Belter, John Henry, 6, 7, 8, 17, 79
   factory, 78
Bergère tabouret, 75
Betty lamp, 136, 137
Biscuit pottery, 195
Bisque, 197
Blown glass, 211
Blown-mold glass, 211
Bohemian glass, 220, 222
Boston and Sandwich Co., 211
Boston rocker, 55, 59, 63, 65, 66
Bristol glass, 220
Britannia ware, 233, 235, 236, 237
   metal, 233

Cabinet Makers' Assistant, The, 3
Candelabra, brass, 142
Candle, 28
Candleholders, 143, 145
   glass dolphin, 146
Cased glass, 220
Chairmakers' Guild, 49
Chairs,
   bergère tabouret, 75
   dating of, 50, 51
   Directoire, 70
   early ladderback design, 30

Chairs—*Continued*
   early Victorian, side, 67
   fancy, 55
   gentleman's, 21, 72, 73, 74, 75
   Hitchcock, 59
   Hitchcock, signed, 60
   imported, 79
   ladies, 21, 72
   Late Empire, 64, 68, 69
   Late Victorian, 19
   Louis XV, 73
   provincial, 49
   Regency, 70
   stenciling of, 56
   Victorian, 59
   Victorian, side, 59, 69
   Windsor, 41, 51, 57
Chests,
   blanket, 90
   Breed and Co., 97
   Civil War period, 93
   columns on, 84
   drawers, 32
   Eastlake, 95
   Empire, 84, 85, 86, 87
   Greek Revival, 84
   John Hall type, 91, 92
   Late American Empire, 85, 96
   Late Victorian, 92
   secretary, 84
   Sheraton, 85
   Victorian, 82
   Victorian provincial, 89
China,
   Faience, 195
   glaze, 195
   hard glaze, 195
   markings, 206
   paste, soft, 195
   pink luster, 194
   soft glaze, 195
Chippendale, Philadelphia, 66
Cipriani, artist, 46
Clark, Heman, 47, 161

INDEX

Clock,
  acorn, 171
  banjo, 165
  bronze, 173
  china, 171
  early brass works, 167
  Empire, 163
  eight-day, 159
  French, 172
  Late Victorian, 166
  ogee, 166, 170
  paper, 160
  papier-mâché, 173
  pilasters, 161
  scrolled, 162
  steeple, 169
  tall, 159
  wag-on-wall, 158
  weights, 159, 168
  wooden works, 156
Coin silverware, 229
Commodes, 104, 105
Corner cupboard, Early Victorian, 106
Cottage furniture, 103
Cranberry glassware, 225
Cup plates,
  historical, 212
  Lacy Sandwich, 212
  Sandwich, 212
Currier, N., 180
Currier and Ives, 23, 180,
  best collectibles, 182
  price of, 183
  reproductions, 183

Daguerreotype, 187
Decanters, 222
Delft, 200
Directoire, French, 40
Domes, glass, 190
Drawers, how made, 32
Drepperd, Carl, *American Pioneer Arts and Artists*, 185
Dresden, 195
Dry sink, 107

Early Victorian, 14
Eastlake, Charles, 14, 17, 18, 20, 72, 97, 103
  Hints on Household Taste in Furniture Upholstery, and Other Details, 18

Eclecticism, Gilman, 11
Empire, American, 40
  era, Late American, 3
  Late, chairs, 68
Engravings, steel, 183

Feet, Chippendale bracket, 41
Footstools, 76
Furniture, dating of, 48

Gaudy Dutch, 203
Gentleman's chairs, 21
German silver, 231
Gilman, 11
Glass,
  blown, 211
  blown mold, 211
  milk white, 213
  pressed, 211
Glassware,
  colored, 218
  cranberry, 225
  Deer and Pine Tree, 218
  maple-leaf pattern, 214
  names of patterns, 226
  pitcher, opalescent coin spot, 220
  Sandwich, 213
  ten most popular forms, 217
  thumb print, 213
Goddard, 20
Godey's *Lady's Book*, 182
Gothic Medieval, 17
Greek Revival, 20
Griswold, Ashbil, 234

Hall, John, furniture design, 2, 4, 5, 6, 17, 68, 91, 94, 97, 100, 114, 124, 126
Haviland, 203
Hepplewhite, 22, 24
Hints on Household Taste in Furniture Upholstery, and Other Details, Charles Eastlake, 18
Hitchcock, Lambert, 46, 58
  chairs, signed, 60
Hoadley, Silas, 158, 160
Hobnail Glassware, 210

Ironstone china, 193
Ives, Joseph, 161, 167

Jarves, Deming, 211, 213
Jerome, Chauncey, 47, 158

244

Lacy Sandwich cup plates, 212
Lady's chairs, 21
Lamps,
  Argand burner, 142
  astral, 145
  Betty, 135
  bracket, 148, 149
  brass mantel, 144
  burning fluid, 137
  Dresden type, 151
  early student, 138
  fairy, 147
  fluid, Porter, 139
  gone-with-the-wind, 155
  grease, 135
  hanging, 155
  Harvard, 153
  Late Victorian, 150
  miniature, 146
  oil, 146
  pewter, 141
  Sandwich glass, 137, 139
  sparking, 140
  student, 138, 151; shades for, 152
  Venetian, 73
  wedding, 149
  wineglass, 140
Lanterns, 143
Late Victorian, 17, 18
Lipman, Jean, *American Primitive Painting*, 185
Locks, drawer, 47
Lotus Ware, 201
Louis XV era, 2, 3
Love seat, 71
Lusters, 224

"Mahoganized" finish, 35
Majolica, 195, 202
Maple-leaf glassware pattern, 216
Marble tops, 105
McKee Bros. 215
Meissen, 195
  onion pattern, 193
Metropolitan Museum Victorian Room, 13
Mid-Victorian, 15, 16, 17
  era, 2, 9, 16, 17, 20
  furnishings in general, 16, 17
Milk white glass, 212, 213

Mirrors,
  dressing, 179
  early, 174
  Empire, 176
  ogee, 176
  rope, 175

Nails,
  machine-made, 31
  modern wire, 31
  old, 29
Napoleon Empire, 2
New England Glass Co., 214, 219
New England Glass Works, 211

Oven, Dutch, 27

Paint, "mahoganized" finish, 35
  old, 35
Paintings on glass, 188
Parian, 192, 197
Paul Revere lantern, 27
Pegs, 29, 34, 45, 50
Pergolesi, artist, 46
Peterson Magazine, 182
Pewter, 231
Philadelphia Centennial, 53
  school, 22
Phoenix Glass Co., 221
Phyfe, Duncan, 2, 20
Picture frames, 189
Pittsburgh glass, 215
Pleat and Panel glassware pattern, 215
Pomona glassware, 219
Porcelain, 192, 193
  Parian-like, 198
Portraits, Victorian, 184
Pottery, biscuit, 195
Pressed glass, 211
Provincial Victorian bedroom, 39
Pulls,
  drawer, carved, 36
  glass, 36
  Late Empire, glass, 37
  Late Victorian, 36
  opalescent, 37
  Sandwich glass, 38
  Victorian, 38

Ramelli, 33
Reed and Barton, 234

Reproductions, 44
  list of, 217
  pattern glassware, 216
Rocker,
  arrow-back, 64
  Boston, 55, 59, 63, 65, 66
  Lincoln, 52, 53, 76
  origin, 62
  Shaker, 52
  stenciled rail, 56
  Windsor, 61
    comb-back, 62
Rocking chair, DeWitt's Patent, 18
Ruby glassware, 223, 224
Rug, Early Victorian, 11
Rural Architecture, Shaw, 9

Sandwich glass, 213, 214
  pulls, 37
Savery, 20
Saw, frame, 43
Saw kerf marks, 33, 41
Saw mill, early, 28
Screws, handmade, 33
  machine made, 34
Secretary,
  John Hall, 100
  Late Victorian, 101
  Provincial Victorian, 98
  Victorian, 99, 101
Semi-china, 195
Settle, Victorian, 54
Shadow boxes, 185, 186
Shaw, *Rural Architecture*, 9
Sheffield plate, 237
Sheraton, 66, 67, 87
Sideboard, Late American Empire, 87, 88
Silver holloware, 236
Silverware,
  Eastlake fashion, 239
  electroplated, 231
  Mid-Victorian, 230
  touchmarks, 232
  Victorian, 228
Sink, dry, 107
Sofa, 80
  Belter, 78
  Grecian, 77
  Victorian, 71

Sperm oil, 137
Spode, 200
Spoons, designs, 238
Staffordshire, 198
Stenciled furniture, 47
Sterling silver, 229
Stoneware, 195

Tables, 109
  American Empire, 113, 115, 117
  bedside, 112
  console, 119, 122
  drop-leaf Empire, 113
  fake reproductions, 45, 118, 119, 120
  Hepplewhite, 115, 122
  hutch, 42
  John Hall design, 114
  Late Empire, 111
  marble top, 123
  Pembroke, 111
  reproductions, 118
  sewing, 110, 111
  Sheraton, 111
  Victorian care, 121
Terry, Eli, 46, 157, 160, 161
Thomas, Seth, 158, 161
Thousand Eye Glassware, 210
Thumbprint glassware pattern, 218
Tiffany glassware, 221
Townsend, 20

Victoria, Queen, 1
Victorian,
  late, 17, 18
  motifs, 9, 10
  Provincial, 26
  silverware, 228
Victorian Room, Metropolitan Museum, 13
Von Stiegel, Baron, glassware, 213

Wedgewood, 199
Whale oil, 137
Whiting, Riley, 47, 158
Willard, Simon, 164
Willow ware, 204
Windsor bench, 57, 58
  rocker, bamboo, 61
Wood, most used in Victorian times, 11